DATE DUE

Mar

MR. CHAIRMAN

THE UNITED STATES CAPITOL

MR. CHAIRMAN

Rules, and examples in story form, of parliamentary procedure

written expressly for use in

SCHOOLS and CLUBS

By

OVETA CULP HOBBY

Former Parliamentarian of the

Texas Legislature

THE ECONOMY COMPANY

Educational Publishers

OKLAHOMA CITY   FORT WORTH   WICHITA   ATLANTA

EDITOR'S FOREWORD

The value of an understanding of parliamentary procedure has come to be recognized as an essential part of one's education. Experience with the training of students in elementary schools, high schools, colleges, social and study clubs, sororities, and fraternities reveals the fact that ordinary school courses fail to bring about a knowledge of the correct usage of parliamentary law.

The author has endeavored to present her own point of view in content and emphasis, but all the suggested usages of parliamentary procedure in this text are in accordance with the best authorities on parliamentary law.

The first part of the text deals with the History of Constitutional Government and Development of Parliamentary Law. This is followed by reading material concerning situations arising in school clubs and societies. The latter part is offered as a guide to those who meet difficulties in the procedure of meetings of various types.

All students need a system of rules to guide them in their home rooms, classes, clubs, assemblies, and in other meetings. The pupils, when serving as officers or on committees, can learn their duties and proper ways of procedure from this conveniently arranged book.

This text no doubt will be used by many adults as a parliamentary guide. In meetings and assemblies of adults the chair should recognize members by their surnames.

The treatise in this book is broad and authentic. It should prove of value for independent study and as a guide to pupils and teachers of the elementary grades, to supervisors and sponsors of high-school and college clubs and to parliamentarians of social and study groups. Thus a needed contribution is made in the field of educational literature.

HARRIET SEAY BINION
Central State Teachers College,
Edmond, Oklahoma.

THE ENGLISH HOUSE OF LORDS

CONTENTS

CONTENTS

CONTENTS

HISTORY OF CONSTITUTIONAL GOVERNMENT
and
DEVELOPMENT OF PARLIAMENTARY LAW

Liberty, which many take as a matter of course, is our most hard-won possession. Countless thousands have died that we might be a free and independent people. The fight for liberty still goes on. To the extent we are forgetful of the origin and growth of our liberties, we become indifferent to guarding them and blind to forces which threaten to take them from us.

Liberty as it is known today is less than eight centuries old. It was born on a little island in the Thames River in South Buckinghamshire, England, or in the adjacent Runnymede meadow. Either the meadow or the island is the spot where the people of England received from a tyrant king the first great document of human liberty, the Magna Charta.

King John, brother to King Richard of the Lion Heart, was perhaps the worst monarch ever to hold the throne of England. Few historians have found anything good to say about John, either as a man or as a ruler. He is known to have been a tyrant, dishonest, untruthful, of violent temper, treacherous and cowardly.

He burdened his people with heavy taxes. He brought foreign soldiers into England to enforce his demands. Sons of leading families were held as hostages, so that their fathers would not attempt to resist him. He plundered the churches.

The people finally could tolerate these conditions no longer. They rebelled. A committee of barons, headed by the Archbishop of Canterbury, presented to King John a series of demands for better government. The king refused to grant their request. The barons assembled their armies. They marched into London where the people welcomed them with rejoicing.

When informed that London had joined the rebels, John agreed to accept the demands of the barons. A meeting was held at Runnymede on June 15, 1215. The king signed the document which we know as the Magna Charta, or great charter. But even after signing it, he delayed handing it over. After four days of waiting, the barons compelled the king to give it to them.

The Magna Charta is the foundation upon which human rights have been built. It is a towering landmark on humanity's long trek to freedom. The ruling power, which until this time had been concentrated in the king, was by it diffused among the people. The king was forced to promise that he no longer would seize or imprison any man or deprive him of life or liberty except by proper trial under the law of the land. Government by law was instituted in England for the first time. Freedom began her long, weary climb to constitutional government. The king was no longer the sole executive, legislative and judicial power of the country.

Among the sixty-three stipulations of the great charter was the first guarantee of religious liberty. Copies of the charter were sent to every cathedral in

England, with orders that it be read to the people twice a year. It was confirmed thirty-two times by subsequent kings.

Had the conditions of the Magna Charta been rigorously observed and defended, there might have been no need for further statement of the rights of men. However, as the years passed, the kings grew more autocratic and the people more indifferent, until abuse once more aroused them in the first quarter of the seventeenth century.

Charles I was king. A weak man, but a tyrant, he was a puppet in the hands of his prime minister, the Duke of Buckingham. Three times within four years Charles dissolved parliament when the representatives of the people refused to grant his wishes.

The disagreement between king and parliament arose over a war with France and Spain which was not sanctioned by the people and was considered by them to be little more than an effort of Charles and Buckingham to obtain personal glory.

Without asking the consent of the people, Charles lodged his soldiers in their homes. When they objected, they were imprisoned. Parliament refused to raise money for the war, but the king ordered a forced loan. Sheriffs and other officials rounded up persons of property and coerced them into lending money to the king, although all knew the loan was not likely to be repaid. Refusal to comply with the king's demands meant imprisonment.

The third parliament passed a bill called the Petition of Right. It declared the acts of the king illegal and ordered that they be discontinued.   Charles at first refused to sign the petition, but parliament held the purse strings, so he was forced to agree, signing it in 1628.

The Petition of Right restated the rights guaranteed in the Magna Charta giving the force of written law to the prohibition of arbitrary imprisonment without trial.   It also banned the lodging of soldiers in private homes and the use of martial law in time of peace.

Until this document was ratified, arbitrary imprisonments were much used by the king and his premier as a method of getting rid of political and personal enemies and to terrorize the people into submission.

The Petition of Right since has become a fundamental part of common law, but after signing it Charles became even more a tyrant.   He dissolved the parliament, imprisoned its leaders, and ruled without parliament for eleven years.   He again raised money by forced loans.

Civil war broke out.   The army of parliament defeated the forces of the king and Charles was tried for murder, tyranny, and treason.   He was convicted and beheaded.

The third of the great documents in the history of liberty is the Writ of Habeas Corpus, enacted by the English parliament in 1679.   The words "habeas corpus" mean "you have the body" and the writ is an order by a court to a person holding another in custody to bring the prisoner into court for a hearing and judgment on the charge.

The Writ of Habeas Corpus is one of the most ancient forms of legal procedure and a magnificent safeguard against tyranny. When enacted by parliament it was not a new principle. It was a restatement of an old principle, which had been violated frequently. The king was one of the chief violators. Ignoring the right of all men to a trial by jury, he would place persons in prison and hold them there without making a formal charge against them. At first it applied only in cases of a criminal nature, but in England in 1816 it was extended to all cases of illegal imprisonment.

The framers of the Constitution of the United States inserted in it the provision that "the privilege of the writ of habeas corpus shall not be suspended unless, when in cases of rebellion or invasion, the public safety may require it."

The fourth great document in the evolution of liberty is the Bill of Rights. Like the other three, it was an outgrowth of differences of opinion between the English people and their king. Unlike the people of some other nations, the English have never accepted as fundamentally true the theory that kings rule by divine right.

They wrested epochal documents from John, Charles I and Charles II. The Bill of Rights was drafted when William and Mary were called to the throne after James II was deposed.

William and Mary accepted the provisions of the Bill of Rights and the document later became the law of the land by parliamentary enactment. It embodied the fundamental principles of human and political liberties.

The eighteenth century saw the fundamental fight for liberty removed from England to the Americas. The

men and women who came to colonize America brought
with them a passionate devotion to the principles of
freedom which their forefathers had at one time established in England. Englishmen, themselves, had become indifferent and the liberties of Englishmen again
were being flouted.

Those who loved liberty came to America because
conditions at home were intolerable. They hoped that
here in America they might enjoy the freedom that obtains where there is no tyranny.

For a while the colonies enjoyed their much-prized
freedom. Soon, however, tyranny began its encroach-
ments. The American Declaration of Independence was
the answer. It is perhaps the most powerful indictment
of tyranny ever voiced by men. In language that de-
fies time and change, it states that the freedom of man
is an inherent right. No words more significant to
mankind were ever penned than these:

"We hold these truths to be self-evident, that all men
are created equal, that they are endowed by their Cre-
ator with certain unalienable Rights, that among these
are Life, Liberty and the pursuit of Happiness,—That
to secure these rights, Governments are instituted
among Men, deriving their just powers from the consent of the governed,—That whenever any Form of
Government becomes destructive of these ends, it is
the Right of the People to alter or to abolish it, and to
institute new Government, laying its foundation on
such principles and organizing its powers in such form,
as to them shall seem most likely to effect their Safety
and Happiness."

A long, bloody war established these principles. Upon this document the American form of government was wrought. As independence from England became assured, the Americans drew up state constitutions embodying many of the principles of the English documents guaranteeing liberty.

In 1787 the states sent delegates to a convention meeting to frame a constitution for the United States. The framers felt that the principles of habeas corpus and of the Bill of Rights were so established in the American concept of government that further statement in the constitution was hardly necessary. The statement that the Writ of Habeas Corpus was not to be suspended except where public safety required it is evidence of that surety.

The Constitution of the United States was submitted to the states for ratification. During the time ratification was taking place the criticism most often heard was that the constitution contained no Bill of Rights. Consequently, ten amendments were drawn up and adopted at one time in 1789 embodying the American Bill of Rights.

These ten articles guarantee to every citizen that he is the political equal of every other citizen. The ten articles are:

Article I.

Congress shall make no law respecting an establishment of religion, or prohibiting the free exercise thereof; or abridging the freedom of speech, or of the press; or the right of the people peaceably to assemble, and to petition the government for a redress of grievances.

Article II.

A well regulated Militia, being necessary to the security of a free State, the right of the people to keep and bear arms shall not be infringed.

Article III.

No Soldier shall, in time of peace be quartered in any house, without the consent of the Owner, nor in time of war, but in a manner to be prescribed by law.

Article IV.

The right of the people to be secure in their persons, houses, papers, and effects, against unreasonable searches and seizures, shall not be violated, and no Warrants shall issue, but upon probable cause, supported by Oath or affirmation, and particularly describing the place to be searched, and the persons or things to be seized.

Article V.

No person shall be held to answer for a capital, or otherwise infamous crime, unless on a presentment or indictment of a Grand Jury, except in cases arising in the land or naval forces, or in the Militia, when in actual service in time of War or in public danger; nor shall any person be subject for the same offence to be twice put in jeopardy of life or limb; nor shall be compelled in any criminal case to be a witness against himself, nor be deprived of life, liberty or property, without due process of law; nor shall private property be taken for public use, without just compensation.

Article VI.

In all criminal prosecutions the accused shall enjoy the right to a speedy and public trial, by an impartial jury of the State and district wherein the crime shall have been committed, which district shall have been previously ascertained by law, and to be informed of the nature and cause of the accusation; to be confronted with the witnesses against him; to have compulsory process for obtaining witnesses in his favor, and to have the Assistance of Counsel for his defence.

Article VII.

In suits at common law, where the value in controversy shall exceed twenty dollars, the right of trial by jury shall be preserved, and no fact tried by a jury shall be otherwise re-examined in any Court of the United States, than according to the rules of the common law.

Article VIII.

Excessive bail shall not be required, nor excessive fines imposed, nor cruel and unusual punishments inflicted.

Article IX.

The enumeration in the Constitution of certain rights shall not be construed to deny or disparage others retained by the people.

Article X.

The powers not delegated to the United States by the Constitution, nor prohibited by it to the States, are reserved to the States respectively, or to the people.

* * *

These amendments, it should never be forgot, constitute a bill of rights, and can not be taken away. At a glance it is obvious that the people of 1789 remembered the victories over tyranny and oppression won by their forbears. They wished to make certain they and their posterity would enjoy the rights so dearly obtained.

In the same atmosphere which produced the Declaration of Independence and the Constitution of the United States, education was freed of its shackles and given recognition as an essential of the maintenance and proper development of democracy.

Thomas Jefferson, from whose pen had flowed the immortal language of the Declaration of Independence, presented to the Virginia legislature in 1779 a bill "for the more general diffusion of knowledge," a measure which recognized for the first time in America the principle that education is a function of the government.

Jefferson believed that an ignorant people are more likely to lose the liberty which is theirs by right than are an educated people. At the time he introduced the bill the colonists still retained the English view that education was the obligation of the family and the business of the church.

Jefferson believed the state should establish an educational system, supported by taxation. As late as 1779 the idea was novel. The masses, it was believed, would become discontented if they were given schools. They might yearn to improve their lot. They might even attempt to change the established order. This was perhaps exactly what Jefferson had in mind when he introduced his "Bill for the more general diffusion of knowledge." The bill recognized public education supported by taxation as a function of government. It outlined a comprehensive school system from elementary school through university. There being no public university, Jefferson designated that students attend William and Mary College at state expense.

The idea was too new. Virginia's legislature defeated the bill. It had, however, a far-reaching influence. Before long state school systems were being established.

A little more than a half century later the Texas Declaration of Independence, adopted March 2, 1836, asserted, "It is an axiom of political science, that unless a people are educated and enlightened, it is idle to expect the continuance of civil liberty, or the capacity for self-government."

Thus a theory which Virginia rejected was a half-century later an axiom!

On an equal footing with other great documents of liberty is a short letter written by George Washington on May 22, 1782, in which he refused to become king. This action probably was one of the principal reasons the United States is today a republic. There seems to be little doubt that Washington could have had a throne, if he had so desired. A great many Americans of the period favored an elective monarchy.

The movement came into the open when Colonel Lewis Nichola, speaking for a group of officers of the Continental army, urged General Washington to become King, or assume the rank of Protector of the

United States. The army was not pleased with the manner in which the continental congress was conducting the affairs of the confederation, and the officers were of the opinion that Washington could overthrow congress much as Napoleon later overthrew the Directoire.

Washington received Nichola's letter with amazement which turned to indignation. He considered it a reflection upon his integrity.

Immediately he called his secretary and dictated his refusal:

"Be assured, Sir," he wrote, "no occurrence in the course of the War has given me more painful sensations than your information of there being such ideas existing in the Army as you have expressed, and I must view with abhorrence, and reprehend with severity. . . .

"I am much at a loss to conceive what part of my conduct could have given encouragement to an address which to me seems big with the greatest mischiefs that can befall my Country . . . . .

"Let me conjure you then, if you have any regard for your Country—concern for yourself or posterity—or respect for me, to banish these thoughts from your mind, and never communicate as from yourself, or anyone else, a sentiment of the like nature."

Washington, reared under a monarchy, knew the evils of power concentrated in the hands of one individual. His refusal to become king and his refusal to serve more than two terms as president were actions which set the young nation firmly on the path of democracy.

Liberty found good soil in the new nation. Rights were outlined in laws which guaranteed their protection. Virginia made several contributions to the establishment of liberty, notable among them an act establishing religious liberty.

The bill was written by Thomas Jefferson and introduced in the Virginia assembly in the same year that he introduced his bill calling for a system of public education. The assembly, however, did not pass it until 1786, seven years later.

"The rights hereby asserted are of the natural rights of mankind, and . . . if any act shall be hereafter passed to repeal the present or to narrow its operation, such act will be an infringement of natural right," the act asserted.

The Supreme Court of the United States later defined the rights of religious freedom in these famous words:

"In this country the full and free right to entertain any religious belief, to practice any religious principle, and to teach any religious doctrine which does not violate the laws of morality and property, and which does not infringe personal rights, is conceded to all. The law knows no heresy, and is committed to the support of no dogma, the establishment of no sect."

All these principles of liberty which were established by our forefathers were incorporated in the American system of government when it was founded. As we have seen, these rights were not won soon or easily.

The Constitution of the United States and its amendments embody these principles. Laws in accord with them are in keeping with the American attitude of freedom. The framers of the constitution knew they could not write a constitution which would serve for all time. They provided a method by which it might be amended, a process which might add further power to the central government, or clarify the rights of the people.

The constitution sets up a triple division of powers of the government. The executive is one branch, the legislative is another and the judicial is the third. This division of power was intended for the safety of the people. They had little liberty, it will be recalled, in the days when the king combined in his person the executive, legislative and judicial branches of government.

The American system of government is free from political tyranny because we have had an independent executive, an independent congress and an independent judicial system. Each acts as a check on and balance for the others.

The success of the people of the United States in overthrowing tyranny also had the effect of inspiring other peoples on the American continents. Republicanism spread like a forest fire. The vast empire which Spain had established in Central and South America rebelled, each unit setting up its own government. And under the Monroe doctrine the United States became the big brother country of the Americas, warning European despots that the Americas henceforth were the home of liberty, no longer a treasure house for foreign oppressors.

Free government is government by just laws. Despotism is government by decree. The laws of a free government are the will of the people, enacted as a guide for the conduct of their business, social and political affairs. The laws of a despotism are the will of one man or a minority and are for the purpose of enslaving the majority.

Throughout the centuries free men have established their laws as the need arose. Set down in their statute books are the laws, or rules of conduct, by which they regulate their lives so that the rights of their neighbors may not be abused.

In open council after free discussion by all interested persons these laws have been enacted. When they are found to infringe upon the rights guaranteed by the documents of liberty, a system by which they may be struck from the books has been provided.

So that order may be maintained in the councils and so that all may be heard and all views registered, we have devised a special set of rules known as parliamentary law. Parliamentary law is made up of rules of procedure which should be used to conduct meetings properly. Just as there are rules of etiquette which should be observed in our every day life; just as we obey traffic rules as an aid to our transportation problems; just as we follow the rules in basketball, football or any other game; so we follow the rules of parliamentary procedure in meetings.

Parliamentary rules are merely the rules of fair play in meetings and organizations. The purpose of these rules is to give every person who wishes to take part in the meetings an opportunity to do so and to insure that the rights of the minority will be respected.

When constitutional government was established and meetings were being held continually to make the laws which would govern the country, it became necessary for the lawmakers to establish a set of rules which would guide the lawmakers in their debate and consideration. So it was that the set of rules known as parliamentary law was made.

Even though the barons who assembled at Runnymede had no knowledge of parliamentary law as we know it today, they had a leader to keep order in their meetings. They were able to come to a decision as to what guarantees of liberty they expected from King John. They were using rules of procedure whether they were called parliamentary rules or not.

Regardless of our purpose in meeting, we must carry on our deliberations in an orderly manner. We must make every effort to see that every member has equal rights with every other member of the meeting. The basis of the American system of government is that every citizen has equal rights before the law. So, in meetings all members should have equal rights of speech.

In every field of life it is necessary to have rules which one observes. In meetings, if the rules are not followed, or if there are no rules, confusion results.

It is easy to see the relation between the age-old struggle for human liberty and the use of parliamentary law. Only through the use of parliamentary law which insures that each member has equal opportunity to express his views in the meeting, can laws be established which will represent the people as a whole.

Every man or woman, boy or girl who desires to be

a good citizen should learn how to take part in a meeting, how to conduct one, and how to protect the rights of the members of the meeting so that all are treated fairly. A knowledge of parliamentary law helps every member of a community to be a better citizen.

The system of procedure known as parliamentary law, like all other great and fundamental rules, was established slowly. Many great minds, such as Thomas Jefferson, contributed to its growth. The orderliness and fairness which it guarantees is the result of a long process of development. Today clubs, organizations and meetings can use the principles of parliamentary law in the knowledge that they are using a well-nigh perfected plan of procedure.

As rules of procedure guided the men who secured the Magna Charta, the Petition of Right, the Writ of Habeas Corpus and the many other great documents which establish human liberties, so will parliamentary law help us through our problems whatever they may be.

In the pages which follow, the author has striven to present the principles of parliamentary law in a simple and understandable manner. This study is an interesting and useful one. A knowledge of parliamentary law is a very helpful tool in present-day life. Organization is the keynote of the American system today; and to take part in organizations one must have the tool of parliamentary law. It is the author's hope that a knowledge of parliamentary law will help you to safeguard the liberty that was won at so great a cost.

CHAPTER I.

THE MASS MEETING

INTRODUCTION

The students in Miss Woods' room at Thomas Jefferson School are studying parliamentary law. They have long been familiar with many details of classroom politeness such as obtaining the permission of the teacher before speaking, speaking about the subject the class is considering instead of interrupting a discussion to bring in some other subject, and voting to learn the wishes of the entire class before taking any action. Now they learn that parliamentary procedure in clubs and organizations is a similar form of good manners for organized groups. Instead of a teacher, a presiding officer, called a president or chairman, keeps order in the group. A member of the group wishing to speak will rise and say "Mr. Chairman," and should not say anything more until the chairman "recognizes" him (calls him by name, thus giving him permission to speak).

Miss Woods: "We must remember that everyone, even the chairman himself, must use the title, 'chairman,' in speaking of the person chosen as chairman. When a member wants the group to do some certain thing he proposes the action to the group in the form of a motion. First he must obtain the floor (be recognized by the chair), then he may introduce his motion by saying 'I move that' or 'I move to' and then stating clearly the one action that he wishes the group to take. For example: 'I move that this club donate $50 from the treasury of the club to the Crippled Children's Fund.' This is known as the main motion or main question. It must be seconded, that is, some one must rise and say 'I second the motion,' but he need not wait for recognition. Until this main question is settled in some way, no one can introduce a different subject.

Sam Hall: "Does everything said in a club need to be in the form of a motion?"

Miss Woods: "The chairman may ask for suggestions and may recognize people and allow them to give their opinions, but until some one makes a definite motion in the form just described, the group cannot debate the subject or take any definite action."

Jean Dallas: "What is debate?"

Miss Woods: "Debate is a discussion of both sides of a question. After a motion has been made and seconded and the chair has repeated it (this is called 'stating the question'), the member who made the motion may obtain recognition and is permitted to speak in favor of the motion. Then others are given recognition and permitted to speak for or against the motion. Not every motion can be debated. You will find a list of undebatable motions in section 142, p. 157 of your textbook."

Jim Wells: "What can be done to a motion besides debating it?"

Miss Woods: "Nina, name one action which an assembly can take concerning a motion other than debating the motion."

Nina Raymond: "It can vote to do the thing described in the motion, can't it?"

Miss Woods: "Yes, it can. If the majority (more than one half) vote 'aye,' the motion is adopted and the organization takes the action proposed in the motion. Not all motions can be adopted by majority vote. Several motions such as amending the constitution and by-laws require a two-thirds vote. Section 159, p. 166 in your text lists these motions. "

Robert Rust: "But suppose a majority should vote 'no'?"

Miss Woods: "Then the motion would be rejected or would fail of adoption. When a motion is rejected it cannot be proposed again in that same session. What can be done to a motion other than debating it and voting on it?"

Clarence Kelley: "Can it be changed?"

Miss Woods: "Yes, it can be amended. What else?"

Ralph Myer: "Can it be turned over to a committee?"

Miss Woods: "Yes, it can be referred to a committee. The motion to refer a proposition to a committee may be worded in several ways—'to commit,' 'to refer,' or if the proposition is being sent back to the committee after having been reported out of committee the motion will be worded 'to re-refer' or 'to recommit.' What other action might an assembly wish to take concerning a motion?"

Lucy Beard: "The assembly might wish to wait to

decide on the motion at some other time. How can that be done, Miss Woods?"

Miss Woods: "The main question can be laid on the table, or it can be postponed to a certain time. Lay on the table, the previous question, postpone to a certain time, commit, amend, and postpone indefinitely are all motions. They are called subsidiary motions and must be made just as main motions are made (requiring recognition and a second). They are made while the main question is being considered and must be disposed of before the main question can be considered again. In sections 162-170, pp. 169-176, in your textbook you will find a description of the various types of motions and an explanation of what is meant by rank and precedence (which is another way of telling how motions affect each other and which can interrupt others)."

Robert Rust: "Miss Woods, when we discuss plans for our class picnic tomorrow as you promised we might, I suggest that we form our own organization and follow the rules we have been studying."

Miss Woods: "Why, Robert, I think that would be a splendid plan. If each of you in the class will read the first chapter in our textbook before class time Monday, I believe you will be able to organize yourselves into a temporary or mass meeting without any difficulty. I suggest that you read also section 149, p. 162.

"Section 8, p. 83 mentions adjournment *sine die*. *Sine die* is a Latin phrase meaning 'without day.' Adjournment *sine die* is adjournment without having set a day for a future meeting. When you have read the

sections mentioned, test yourself by trying to define
these terms:

Obtain recognition
Lay on the table
Obtain the floor
Postpone to a certain time
Mr. Chairman
Adopt
Motion
Reject
Subsidiary motion
Majority
Amend
Debate
Commit."

MASS MEETING PROCEDURE

(In room 19 with Miss Woods, teacher, at the desk.)

Miss Woods: "The meeting will please come to order.
(Waits for silence.)   This meeting has been called to
make plans for the picnic and nominations are now in
order for a chairman."

Jane Lee (rises and addresses Miss Woods): "Madam
Chairman."

The Chair: "Jane."

Jane: "I move that John Rogers be elected chairman
of this meeting."

Ralph Myer: "I second the motion."*

---

*Nominations do not require a second, but seconding the nomination
is permitted in most organizations as a courtesy to the nominee.

Robert Rust: "Madam Chairman."

The Chair: "Robert."

Robert: "I nominate Sam Hall."

Mary Randall: "I second the nomination."

The Chair: "Are there any further nominations? (If, after waiting a reasonable time, no further nominations are made and no motion is made to close nominations, she may continue.) As many as favor the election of John Rogers as chairman will stand. (She makes the count.) Those opposed to John Rogers will stand. (She makes the count.) There being seven ayes and thirty-three noes, John Rogers fails to be elected."

The Chair: "As many as favor the election of Sam Hall will stand. (She makes the count.) Those opposed to Sam Hall will stand. (She makes the count.) There being thirty-three ayes and seven noes, Sam Hall has received a majority of the votes cast and is elected chairman of this meeting." (Miss Woods leaves the chair and Sam Hall takes her place as chairman or presiding officer of the meeting. He must now be addressed as "Mr. Chairman." Miss Woods takes a seat near the chairman and acts as parliamentarian.)

The Chair: "Nominations are now in order for a secretary."

Robert Rust: "Mr. Chairman."

The Chair: "Robert."

Robert: "I move that Mary Randall be elected secretary."

Alice Felton: "I second the motion."

The Chair: "Are there any further nominations?"

Clarence Kelley: "Mr. Chairman."

The Chair: "Clarence."

Clarence: "I nominate Jane Lee."

John Rogers: "I second the nomination."

The Chair: "Are there any further nominations? (No one speaks. If, after waiting a reasonable time, no motion is made to close nominations, he may continue.) As many as favor the election of Mary Randall as secretary will rise and stand until counted. (He makes the count.) As many as favor the election of Jane Lee will rise and stand until counted."

Parliamentarian: "Mr. Chairman."

The Chair: "Miss Woods."

Parliamentarian: "You failed to complete the question on the first nomination. Even though you may be certain the candidate did not receive a majority of votes, it is necessary to state the negative side of the question."*

The Chair: "Those opposed to Mary Randall as secretary will rise and stand until counted. (He makes the count.) There being seventeen ayes and twenty-three noes, Mary Randall fails to be elected."

The Chair: "As many as favor the election of Jane Lee will rise and stand until counted. (He makes the count.) Those opposed to Jane Lee will rise and stand until counted. (He makes the count.) There being twenty-three ayes and seventeen noes, Jane Lee has received a majority of the votes cast and is elected secretary of the meeting." (Jane sits near the chairman and keeps minutes, a record of what is done in the meeting.)

---

*In ordinary procedure suggestions or criticisms by the parliamentarian are addressed to the chair and are not heard by the assembly, but, in order that the students may have the benefit of the criticism, the parliamentarian has here made it aloud.

The Chair: "As you know, this meeting has been called to decide the date and make arrangements for our picnic. What date do the members think best? The chair will be glad to hear suggestions."

Jean: "Mr. Chairman."

The Chair: "Jean."

Jean: "I move that the picnic be held on May 15."

Clarence Kelley: "I second the motion."

The Chair: "It has been moved and seconded that the picnic be held on May 15. As many as favor the motion will say 'aye.' (A number say 'aye.') Those opposed to holding the picnic on May 15 will say 'no.' (A number say 'no.') The chair is in doubt about the vote. Will those in favor of May 15 please rise and stand until counted. Will the secretary please make the count."

Secretary (speaking to the chair): "Twenty-three."

The Chair: "Will those opposed to May 15 please rise and stand until counted? Will the secretary please make the count?"

Secretary (speaking to the chair): "Seventeen."

The Chair: "There being twenty-three ayes and seventeen noes, the motion is carried and the picnic will be held on May 15."

The Chair: "We must next discuss where we shall have the picnic. Are there any suggestions?"

Bertha Jones: "Mr. Chairman."

The Chair: "Bertha."

Bertha: "I suggest Laurel Lake."

Martin West: "Mr. Chairman."

The Chair: "Martin."

Martin: "How about Winfield's Grove?"

Grover Thomas: "Mr. Chairman."

The Chair: "Grover."

Grover: "I move that the chair appoint a committee of three persons to recommend a place."

Bertha Jones: "I second the motion."

The Chair: "It has been moved and seconded that the chair appoint a committee of three persons to recommend a place for the picnic. As many as favor the appointment of such committee will say 'aye.' (A large number say 'aye.') Those opposed will say 'no.' (A few say 'no.')"

The Chair: "The motion has carried and the chair appoints Grover Thomas, Bertha Jones and Ralph Myer; Grover Thomas will be chairman of the committee. If there is no objection, the committee will retire to consider the question."

The Chair: "We must next consider the method of transportation."

Robert Rust: "Mr. Chairman."

The Chair: "Robert."

Robert: "I move that the chair appoint a committee of five to recommend arrangements for transportation."

Alice Felton: "I second the motion."

The Chair: "It has been moved and seconded that the chair appoint a committee of five to recommend arrangements for transportation. As many as favor the motion will say 'aye.' (A large number say 'aye.') Those opposed will say 'no.' (No one speaks.) The motion is carried and the chair appoints Alice Felton, Robert Rust, Tom Barnes, John Rogers and Jean Dallas. If there is no objection the committee will retire to consider the question."

John Rogers: "Mr. Chairman."

The Chair: "John."

John: "The chair forgot to name the chairman of the committee."

The Chair: "No, the chair did not forget. The committee may select its own chairman when it meets."

(The committee withdraws. The committee named to recommend a place for the picnic having returned to the assembly hall, the chairman rises to speak.)

Grover Thomas: "Mr. Chairman."

The Chair: "Grover."

Grover: "The committee named to recommend a place for the picnic is ready to report."

The Chair: "We will hear the report."

Grover (reading): "Mr. Chairman, we, your committee appointed to recommend a place for the picnic, recommend Laurel Lake.

Grover Thomas

Bertha Jones

Ralph Myer."

The Chair: "You have heard the recommendation of the committee. Is there a motion?"

Nina Raymond: "Mr. Chairman."

The Chair: "Nina."

Nina: "I move that the picnic be held at Laurel Lake."

Jim Wells: "I second the motion."

The Chair: "As many as favor having the picnic at Laurel Lake will say 'aye.' (A large number say 'aye.')

Those opposed will say 'no.' (A few scattered noes are heard.) The ayes have it and the picnic will be held at Laurel Lake."

(The committee on transportation having returned to the assembly hall, the chairman rises to speak.)

John Rogers: "Mr. Chairman."

The Chair: "John."

John: "Your committee on transportation is ready to report."

The Chair: "We will hear the report."

John: "Mr. Chairman, the committee on transportation begs to report that enough cars have been promised by members of the class to carry the entire group to the picnic and they will be in front of the school at eight o'clock on the morning of May 15.

John Rogers, Chairman."

Tom Jones: "Mr. Chairman."

The Chair: "Tom."

Tom Jones: "I move that the class make use of the cars arranged for by the committee on transportation."

Jim Wells: "I second the motion."

The Chair: "It has been moved and seconded that the class make use of the cars arranged for by the committee on transportation. As many as favor the motion will say 'aye.' (A large number say 'aye.') As many as are opposed to the motion will say 'no.' (No one speaks.) The motion is unanimously adopted. Members of the class will please take note of the arrangements made by the committee and meet at eight o'clock, on the morning of May 15 in front of the school building."

The Chair: "Is there any further business to come before the assembly?" (Pause.)

Secretary: "Mr. Chairman."

The Chair: "Jane."

Secretary: "If there is no further business to come before the assembly, I should like to read the minutes."*

The Chair: "Read the minutes, please."

Secretary (reading):

"Minutes of Mass Meeting, April 5, 19—.

"Miss Woods' class met in Room 19 on Monday, April 5, 19—, at two o'clock p. m. for the purpose of perfecting plans for a picnic. Miss Woods presided. Sam Hall was elected chairman, and Jane Lee, secretary.

"A motion was made by Jean Dallas and seconded by Clarence Kelley that May 15 be chosen. The motion was adopted.

"The place for the picnic was next discussed. It was moved by Grover Thomas and seconded by Bertha Jones that the chair appoint a committee of three to recommend the place. Grover Thomas, Bertha Jones and Ralph Myer were appointed on this committee, Grover Thomas being appointed chairman.

"On a motion by Robert Rust, seconded by Alice Felton, the chair appointed a committee of five, Alice Felton, Robert Rust, Tom Barnes, John Rogers and Jean Dallas, to recommend arrangements for transportation.

"The chairman of the committee appointed to recommend a place for the picnic read the report which

---

*See footnote, Section 8, page 84.

recommended Laurel Lake. Upon a motion by Nina Raymond, seconded by Jim Wells, Laurel Lake was chosen.

"John Rogers, chairman of the committee on transportation, reported that the committee had secured the promise of enough cars to carry the class to Laurel Lake. A motion was made by Tom Jones, seconded by Jim Wells, that the class make use of the cars arranged for by the committee on transportation. The motion carried.

Jane Lee, Secretary."

The Chair: "You have heard the reading of the minutes. Are there any corrections? (Pause.) If not, they stand approved as read."

The Chair: "Is there any further business to come before the assembly? (Pause.) If not, is there a motion to adjourn?"

Clarence Kelley: "Mr. Chairman."

The Chair: "Clarence."

Clarence: "I move that this assembly do now adjourn."

Ben Rice: "I second the motion."

The Chair: "It has been moved and seconded that the assembly adjourn. As many as favor the motion will say 'aye.' (A full vote is indicated, but the chair completes the question.) Those opposed will say 'no.' " (No one speaks.)

The Chair: "The assembly stands adjourned *sine die*."

CHAPTER II.

ORGANIZATION OF A PERMANENT SOCIETY

INTRODUCTION

(It is the day after the temporary or mass meeting. Miss Woods has asked the members of the class to write any questions or comments they may have in mind concerning the meeting of the day before. Robert Rust takes a sheet of paper from his desk and passes it to the students sitting near him. Each student reads it and signs his name. Finally it is handed to Miss Woods.)

Miss Woods (reading aloud):

" 'To Miss Woods:

We, the undersigned, do respectfully petition that permission be given to organize this class into a dramatic club for the purpose of reading and presenting plays under the direction of a competent director.

Respectfully submitted,'

(She folds the paper.)

"I shall not read the names attached because I see that almost every member of the class has signed. This petition is in excellent form and I shall be glad to grant my permission. It is customary for those interested in forming a permanent society to talk over the matter, and to issue a call for a temporary or mass meeting to consider the matter and to form a permanent organization. Being one of the interested group, I invite you to meet me here at class time tomorrow to consider organizing ourselves into a dramatic club for the purpose of reading and presenting plays under a competent director.

"Before the first meeting, it is well for those issuing the call to plan the type of organization which will best carry out their plans. They should study the constitution and rules of other organizations of the same type to help them plan their own organization."

David Fox: "Miss Woods, the textbook mentions resolutions. What is a resolution?"

Miss Woods: "A motion of especial importance should be put in writing. It is then called a resolution. For form of a resolution, read section 85, p. 128-31 in your text and notice the form of resolution given after the committee report. A committee or an individual may give a favorable opinion of a certain action, but unless that opinion is put in the form of a motion or a resolution it cannot be debated nor voted upon.

"It is customary for the plan of the organization to be introduced by a resolution. The resolution should tell something of the organization, its aims and purpose. This resolution can be drawn by a committee appointed during the temporary meeting, or some one may write a resolution or set of resolutions before he comes to the meeting and offer it from the floor."

Margaret Richards: "In the temporary meeting yesterday we adjourned *sine die*. How should this temporary meeting to form a permanent organization adjourn?"

Miss Woods: "When a mass or temporary meeting is held for the purpose of forming a permanent organization, the organization provides for another meeting which is called an adjourned meeting. This can be accomplished by either of two motions. Inasmuch as this temporary organization contemplates forming a permanent organization, the proper motion to make is either the privileged motion to fix the time to which to adjourn or a motion to adjourn which is qualified by naming a time for reassembling."

Alice Felton: "What is the meaning of the word 'precedence' describing a motion?"

Miss Woods: "There are several classifications of motions. Since several motions may be pending at one time, it is necessary that certain motions be considered before others. Precedence, as it is used in parliamentary law, means the rank of the various motions.

"The motion to adjourn may be pending when another member makes a motion to fix the time to which to adjourn. The latter motion is of higher rank than the motion to adjourn and must be disposed of before the organization can again consider the motion to adjourn. The precedence of motions is explained in section 170, p. 175 of your text."

Harry Fisher: "In organizing a dramatic club tomorrow, should we elect permanent officers first or adopt a constitution first?"

Miss Woods: "The constitution must be adopted before there is any authority to elect permanent officers. The constitution will provide for the number and rank of officers to be elected. The temporary organization will have a temporary chairman and a temporary secretary.

"Before class time tomorrow read sections 10-15, pp. 84-88 on permanent societies, and sections 21-28, pp. 92-101 on constitution and by-laws. You might try to learn more about motions before tomorrow also, and be thinking about the duties of officers.

"Be sure that you understand thoroughly the following parliamentary terms:

Petition
Constitution
By-laws
Resolution
Fix time to which to adjourn
Adjourned meeting
Precedence."

TEMPORARY MEETING TO ORGANIZE A PERMANENT SOCIETY

(In room 19 with Miss Woods, teacher, at the desk.)

Miss Woods: "The meeting will please come to order. (Waits for silence.) Some of the class have asked that we organize a dramatic club and this meeting has been called to discuss the matter. Nominations are now in order for a temporary chairman."

Betty Abbott (obtains recognition): "I nominate Leon Camp for chairman."

Carrie Adkins: "I second the nomination."

Bob Hunter (obtains recognition): "I move nominations be closed."

Bill Daniel: "I second the motion."

The Chair: "Remember a motion to close nominations requires a two-thirds vote. As many as are in favor of closing nominations will rise and stand until counted. (Votes are counted.) Those opposed to closing nominations will rise and stand until counted. (Votes are counted.) There being thirty-four ayes and six noes, the motion is carried and nominations are closed. As many as favor Leon Camp for chairman will rise and stand until counted. (Votes are counted.) Those opposed to Leon Camp for chairman will rise and stand until counted. (No one stands.) There being no opposition, Leon Camp is unanimously elected chairman." (Leon now takes the chair and Miss Woods acts as parliamentarian.)

The Chair: "Nominations are now in order for a secretary."

Bill Daniel (obtaining recognition): "I nominate Lucy Beard for secretary."

Harry Fisher: "I second the nomination."

Bob Hunter (obtaining recognition): "I nominate Nell Talley."

Joe Lucas: "I second the nomination."

The Chair: "Are there any further nominations?

(No one speaks. The chairman waits a reasonable time.) As many as favor Lucy Beard for secretary will rise and stand until counted. (Votes are counted.) Those opposed to Lucy Beard for secretary will rise and stand until counted. (Votes are counted.) There being thirty ayes and ten noes, Lucy Beard is elected secretary." (Lucy takes a seat near the chairman and keeps a record of the proceedings.)

The Chair: "Some of us have been talking about organizing a dramatic club and giving a play every two or three months and we thought that since we are studying parliamentary law we ought to be able to carry out some of the things we have learned from it in organizing the club. I should like to hear what some of the rest of the class think about this."

David Fox (obtaining recognition): "I do not know about giving plays, but I think it would be fun to have a club where we can practice some of the things we have been learning. I plan to be a lawyer and I may go to the legislature some day. Then I would need to know how to do things."

George McNeil (obtaining recognition): "Seems to me if we organize a club and have regular meetings and officers and carry it on like a real club that we would do most of the things they do in the legislature."

Margaret Richards (obtaining recognition): "If we have a dramatic club we could practice using parliamentary rules in the regular meetings of the club and when we give a play we could have some one help us present it. I should think learning how to speak would be the very thing for anyone who wants to be a lawyer."

Agnes Sanders (obtaining recognition): "I think it is a good idea, I wish we would organize a dramatic club."

The Chair: "Will you put that in the form of a motion?"

Agnes: "I move that Room 19 organize a dramatic club to study and present plays."

Margaret Richards: "I second the motion."

The Chair: "It has been moved and seconded that Room 19 organize a dramatic club for the purpose of studying and presenting plays. Is there any discussion? (Waits for discussion. No one speaks.) As many as favor the motion will say 'aye.' (There is a large vote.) Those opposed will say 'no.' (No one votes.) The ayes have it and the motion is carried.

"A motion is now in order that a committee be appointed to prepare a constitution and by-laws."

Harry Fisher (obtaining recognition): "I move that the chair appoint a committee of five to prepare a constitution and by-laws."

Bob Hunter: "I second the motion."

The Chair: "It has been moved and seconded that the chair appoint a committee of five to prepare a constitution and by-laws. As many as favor the motion will say 'aye.' (There is a large vote.) Those opposed will say 'no.' (No one votes.) The motion is carried and the chair appoints David Fox, George McNeil, Betty Abbott, Margaret Richards and Bill Daniel as a committee to prepare a constitution and by-laws."

The Chair: "If there is no further business to come

before the assembly a motion to adjourn is in order."

Ethel Pierce (obtaining recognition): "I move that we adjourn until next Friday at two o'clock p. m."

Agnes Sanders: "I second the motion."

The Chair: "It has been moved and seconded that the club adjourn until next Friday at two o'clock p. m. As many as favor the motion will say 'aye.' (There is a large vote.) Those opposed will say 'no.' (No one speaks.) The motion is carried and the club stands adjourned until next Friday at two o'clock p. m."

DISCUSSION OF CONSTITUTION AND BY-LAWS

Miss Woods: "I am glad that all the members of the committee on constitution and by-laws are in class today. Perhaps we can help them to draft a useful constitution."

Joe Lucas: "How do constitutions, by-laws, standing rules, and rules of order differ?"

Miss Woods: "You might compare these four classes of rules and their share in the building of an organization to the building of a house. First you must lay your foundation firmly. It cannot easily be changed later. This foundation is the constitution with its provisions for name, purpose, officers, membership, and other essentials.

"Then the walls are built on the foundation following it closely in shape. These also are permanent and are not easily changed. These are the by-laws.

"When we move into a house it must have walls and foundation; when we organize a club we must adopt a constitution and by-laws before we can transact any business as an organization. Later we can add standing rules and rules of order as we need them. They are like pieces of furniture: they are necessary but they can be moved or taken away without disturbing the foundation and walls, or in the case of a club, the constitution and by-laws.

"What other questions do you wish to ask concerning the constitution?"

Betty Abbott: "Our text says that officers must be elected by ballot. What does that mean?"

Miss Woods: "Voting by ballot is done by having each member write his vote on a slip of paper. If it is an election, he writes the name of the person he wishes to elect. The member may vote for one of the persons nominated or write in any other name he wishes."

Nell Talley: "In our temporary meeting we elected by saying 'aye' or 'no.' Is that what the textbook means by '*viva voce* vote'?"

Miss Woods: "Yes, it is. Then there are other methods of voting. How does a chairman know which to use?"

Ethel Pierce: "Some member may make a motion to decide what method to use."

Miss Woods: "Yes, that is the motion to fix the method of voting discussed in section 237, p. 256 and section 173, p. 179. When no motion is made, the chairman may take a *viva voce* vote. If he is in doubt as to whether ayes or noes have it or if any one member doubts the result of the vote, the chair asks the ayes to stand until counted, then the noes to stand until counted. This is called division of the house. What method of voting does your textbook give that we have failed to mention?"

Margaret Richards: "Voting by roll call."

Miss Woods: "That is the one. Raising of hands is just another form of division. Voting by roll call is usually called for by several members. The by-laws or rules of order should provide the number of persons required to call for a vote by roll call. What further questions do you wish to ask concerning constitutions and by-laws?"

Tom Barnes: "Suppose we do not like the constitution the committee writes, what can we do about it?"

Miss Woods: "You can amend it. The constitution will be read once as a whole, then again one paragraph at a time. After a paragraph is read any member may make a motion to amend that paragraph. This amendment may be debated after it is stated by the chair, and may itself be amended. Open your books to section 13, p. 86 and see how amendments may be made. (She waits for them to read the section.) Notice that after each paragraph is read amendments may be made and voted on but the paragraph itself as amended is not voted on. After opportunity has been given to amend each paragraph, the chair asks if there are any amendments to the constitution as a whole. This opportunity to amend the constitution as a whole presents a chance for the group to amend an earlier paragraph of the constitution to conform to the sense of a later paragraph which has been amended, or to add a new paragraph or to strike out a paragraph previously considered.

When no further amendments are offered or when debate has been cut off, the question is on the adoption of the constitution."

Walter Taylor: "Why is a majority vote large enough to amend the constitution before it is adopted as a whole when a two-thirds vote is required to amend the constitution after it has been adopted?"

Miss Woods: "Before a constitution is adopted, an amendment or an amendment to the amendment can be adopted by a majority vote for the reason that the constitution before adoption is just a resolution presented by a committee. The group may vote against the entire constitution recommended by the committee, or any part of it, but after a constitution is adopted it becomes the organic law and any amendment to it requires previous notice and a two-thirds vote.

"Before our organization meeting tomorrow you might check to be sure that you understand how to amend and to adopt a constitution. I suggest that you read again with especial care the procedure outlined in section 13, p. 86. You may use that procedure in adopting either the constitution or the by-laws."

FIRST ADJOURNED MEETING

(In Room 19 with Leon Camp, temporary chairman, in the chair.)

The Chair: "The meeting will please come to order. The secretary will call the roll."

(The secretary calls the roll. The names of two absent members are noted in the minutes.)

THE SEVENTY-FOURTH CONGRESS IN SESSION

Copyright by Harris & Ewing

The Chair: "The secretary will read the minutes."

Secretary:

"Minutes of Meeting Called to Organize a Dramatic Club, Wednesday, April 7, 19—.

"The students of Room 19 met in their home room Wednesday, April 7, 19—, at two o'clock p. m., for the purpose of organizing a dramatic club. Miss Woods presided.

"Leon Camp was elected temporary chairman, and Lucy Beard, temporary secretary.

"After an informal discussion a motion was introduced by Agnes Sanders, and seconded by Margaret Richards, that Room 19 form a dramatic club for the purpose of studying and presenting plays. The motion was adopted.

"A motion was introduced by Harry Fisher and seconded by Bob Hunter that the chair appoint a committee of five to prepare a constitution and by-laws. The motion was adopted and David Fox, George McNeil, Betty Abbott, Margaret Richards and Bill Daniel were appointed on this committee.

"A motion was made by Nell Talley, and seconded by Agnes Sanders, that the club adjourn until Friday, April 9, 19—, at two o'clock, p. m. The motion was adopted.

Lucy Beard, Secretary."

The Chair: "You have heard the reading of the minutes. Are there any corrections?"

Agnes Sanders (obtaining recognition): "It was Ethel Pierce who made the motion to adjourn."

The Chair: "Is there any objection to making the correction? (The chairman pauses.) Are there any other corrections? If not, the minutes stand approved with this correction."

Bill Daniel (obtaining recognition): "The committee on constitution and by-laws is ready to report."

The Chair: "Read your report."

Bill: "Mr. Chairman:

"The committee on constitution and by-laws appointed by you begs leave to submit the following constitution and by-laws and recommends their adoption.
Bill Daniel, Chairman."

(He sends the constitution and by-laws to the chairman who hands them to the secretary and asks her to read the constitution.)

Secretary: "Mr. Chairman:

"CONSTITUTION OF THE GREEN LANTERN DRAMATIC CLUB

Article I. Name

The name of this club shall be Green Lantern Dramatic Club.

Article II. Object

The object of this organization shall be to study and present plays.

Article III. Membership

Section 1. Membership in this organization shall be limited to two classes, active and associate. The membership shall be composed of persons in the Thomas Jefferson School.

Section 2.   A majority of the members shall elect additional members.

Section 3.   Active members shall attend at least one-half of the regular meetings and be responsible for the presentation of dramas selected by the club.

Section 4.   Associate members shall be chosen from the faculty and shall be entitled to all the privileges of the club except those of voting and holding office: however, they shall not be held responsible for the presentation of dramas.

Article IV.   Officers

Section 1.   The officers of this organization shall be a president, a vice-president, a secretary, a treasurer and a parliamentarian.

Section 2.   All officers of this organization shall be elected by ballot at the annual meeting and shall hold office until the next annual election or until their successors are elected.

Section 3.   A majority of all votes cast shall be necessary to constitute an election.

Section 4.   Vacancies in office shall be filled by special election.

Article V.   Quorum

One-third of the active membership of the organization shall constitute a quorum.

Article VI.   Meetings

Section 1.   The annual meeting of the organization shall be held on the third Friday in May.

Section 2. Regular meetings shall be held on the first Friday of each month.

Section 3. Special meetings shall be called by the president, or by the vice-president in the absence of the president, or by any five members of the club.

Article VII.   Nominating Committee

The nominating committee shall be appointed by the president not later than the first Friday in April. It shall consist of five members of the organization.

Article VIII.   Authority in Parliamentary Law

This organization shall be governed by Hobby's 'Mr. Chairman.'

Article IX.   Amendments

This constitution may be amended at any regular meeting; provided, however, that the amendments shall have been submitted at the last regular meeting in writing, and that the adoption of the amendments hereto shall require a two-thirds vote."

The Chair: "It may be that there will be some paragraphs in the constitution which the club will not approve and, if so, we will discuss these sections and amend or omit them, but before we can do this a motion must be made favoring the adoption of the proposed constitution."

Walter Taylor (obtaining recognition): "I move that the constitution be adopted."

Nell Talley: "I second the motion."

The Chair: "It has been moved and seconded that the constitution be adopted. The Secretary will read Article I."

Secretary (reading): "Article I. Name. The name of this club shall be Green Lantern Dramatic Club."

Agnes Sanders (obtaining recognition): "I move that 'Article I' be amended by striking out the words 'Dramatic Club' and inserting in their place the word 'Players.'"

Bob Hunter (obtaining recognition): "I thought that was what we are organizing so I do not see what is wrong with calling it a dramatic club."

Parliamentarian (in an aside to the chair): "Until a motion has been seconded and stated by the chair it is out of order to debate the question."

The Chair: "The parliamentarian reminds me that until the question has been seconded and stated, debate is not in order. Is there a second to the motion?"

Betty Abbott: "I second the motion."

The Chair: "It has been moved and seconded that 'Article I' be amended by striking out the words, 'Dramatic Club' and inserting the word 'Players.' Is there any discussion?"

Jane Lee (obtaining recognition): "I like the word 'Players' better, myself. 'Green Lantern Dramatic Club' is too long and until we have had some experience I think it would sound better just to call ourselves 'Players.'"

Joe Lucas (obtaining recognition): "By the end of the year when we have given several plays we shall have plenty of experience."

David Fox (obtaining recognition): "I move the previous question on the amendment to Article I."

Bill Daniel: "I second the motion."

Carrie Adkins: "Mr. Chairman."

The Chair: "For what purpose do you seek recognition?"

Carrie: "To speak on the amendment."

The Chair: "After a motion for the previous question has been made and seconded further debate is out of order unless the motion for the previous question fails.

"The previous question has been moved and seconded on the pending amendment. As many as favor ordering the previous question on the pending amendment will stand and be counted. This motion requires a two-thirds vote for adoption. (The chairman pauses for the count.) Those opposed to ordering the previous question on the pending amendment will stand until counted. (The votes are counted.) There being thirty ayes and eight noes, the motion has carried and the question is now on the proposed amendment, which requires only a majority vote. As many as favor amending Article I by striking out the words 'Dramatic Club' and inserting in their place the word 'Players' will say 'aye.' (There is a large vote.) Those opposed will say 'no'. (There is a small vote.) The motion is carried and the amendment is adopted. The secretary will read Article II."

Secretary (reading): "Article II. Object. The object of this organization shall be to study and present plays."

Betty Abbott (obtaining recognition): "I move that Article II be amended by adding the words 'under a competent director and casting committee.' "

Nell Talley: "I second the motion."

The Chair: "It has been moved and seconded that 'Article II' be amended by adding the words 'under a competent director and casting committee.' Is there any discussion?"

David Fox (obtaining recognition): "I move to amend the amendment by adding the words 'chosen from the associate members.'"

Tom Barnes: "I second the motion."

The Chair: "The question is on the adoption of the amendment to the amendment, adding the words 'chosen from the associate members.' Is there any discussion? (No one speaks.) As many as favor amending the amendment by adding the words 'chosen from the associate members' will say 'aye.' (There is a small vote.) Those opposed to amending the amendment by adding the words 'chosen from the associate members' will say 'no.' (There is a large vote.) The motion is lost. The question is now on the adoption of the amendment. Is there any discussion? (No one speaks.) As many as favor the adoption of the amendment adding the words 'under a competent director and casting committee will say 'aye'. (There is a large vote.) Those opposed to the adoption of the amendment will say 'no'. (No one speaks.) The ayes have it and the amendment is adopted. The secretary will read Article III section by section.'"

Secretary (reading): "Article III. Membership.
Section 1. Membership in this organization shall be limited to two classes, active and associate. The membership shall be composed of persons in the Thomas Jefferson School."

The Chair: "Is there any discussion?" (No one speaks.)

Secretary (reading): "Section 2. A majority of the members shall elect additional members."

The Chair: "Is there any discussion?" (No one speaks.)

(The secretary continues to read the constitution article by article and section by section, and after each section is read the chair invites discussion. All of the constitution is read.)

The Chair: "The constitution is now open to amendment as a whole. Is there any discussion?" (No one speaks.)

The Chair: "The question is on the adoption of the constitution as amended. Are you ready for the question?" (No one speaks.)

The Chair: "As many as favor the adoption of the constitution as amended will stand until counted. (The chairman pauses for the count.) Those opposed to the adoption of the constitution as amended will stand until counted. (The chairman pauses for the count.) There being thirty-four ayes and four noes, the motion has carried and the constitution is adopted. The secretary will now read the by-laws."

Secretary (reading):

"BY-LAWS OF THE GREEN LANTERN PLAYERS
Article I. Dues

The dues of the Green Lantern Players shall be twenty-five cents a year, payable at the annual meeting for the following year.

Article II. Duties of Officers

Section 1. The president shall preside at all meetings when he is present. He shall appoint all committees, standing and special.

Section 2. The vice-president shall preside at the meetings in the absence of the president. He shall be chairman of the committee on selection of plays.

Section 3. The secretary shall keep an accurate record of the meetings, attend to all correspondence assigned to him, act as custodian for all materials to be used by committees, keep an up-to-date membership list, and keep a record of the attendance.

Section 4. The treasurer shall keep a faithful account of all money received and expended and shall report annually to the organization. He shall keep his books up to date and be prepared to give a report at any time requested by the president.

Article III. Committees

Section 1. There shall be three standing committees: committee on selection of plays, committee on finance, and committee on membership.

Section 2. The committee on selection of plays shall read and recommend the plays to be given by the club.

Section 3. The committee on finance shall attend to all matters regarding money and shall report to the organization at the annual meeting or when called upon by the president.

Section 4. The committee on membership shall vouch for all new persons who are offered for membership.

Article IV.   Meetings

The regular meetings of the organization shall be held at two o'clock p. m. on the first Friday of each month.

Article V.   Order of Business

The organization shall conduct business in the following order:

1. Call to order
2. Roll call
3. Excuses for absent members
4. Reading of minutes
5. Report of the treasurer
6. Reports of standing committees
7. Reports of special committees
8. Unfinished business
9. New business
10. Adjournment.

Article VI.   Suspension

The suspension of any part of these by-laws shall require a two-thirds vote of the members present.

Article VII.   Amendment

These by-laws may be amended at any regular meeting, provided that notice of proposed amendments has been given. Such amendments shall require a two-thirds vote of the members present for adoption."

The Chair: "Is there a motion favoring the adoption of the by-laws?"

Walter Taylor (obtaining recognition): "I move that the by-laws be adopted."

Joe Lucas: "I second the motion."

The Chair: "It has been moved and seconded that the by-laws be adopted. The secretary will now read the by-laws paragraph by paragraph."

Secretary (reading): "Article I. Dues. The dues of the Green Lantern Players shall be twenty-five cents per year, payable at the annual meeting for the following year."

Ben Rice (obtaining recognition): "I move that the section be amended by striking out the words 'twenty-five cents' and inserting in their place the words 'thirty-five cents.'"

Harry Fisher: "I second the motion."

The Chair: "It has been moved and seconded that Article I be amended by striking out the words 'twenty-five cents' and inserting in their place the words 'thirty-five cents.' Is there any discussion?"

Bob Hunter (obtaining recognition): "I do not see why we should make the dues so high. Twenty cents should be enough."

Nell Talley (obtaining recognition): "We are going to need money for a good many things before we give our first play and I think we should make it fifty cents."

The Chair: "If there is no objection, we will consider the amount to be inserted in the amendment as a blank and those wishing to suggest different amounts to fill the blank may write these amounts on slips of paper and give them to the secretary. (Several hand slips to the secretary.) We shall vote on the largest amount suggested first. As many as favor filling the blank with the words 'fifty cents' will say 'aye'. (There is a small vote.) Those opposed will say 'no'. (There is

a large vote.)   The noes have it and the motion fails.
As many as favor filling the blank with the words
'thirty-five cents' will say 'aye'.   (There is a small vote.)
Those opposed to filling the blank with the words 'thirty-
five cents' will say 'no'.   (There is a large vote.)   The
noes have it and the motion fails.   As many as favor
filling the blank with the words 'thirty cents' will say
'aye'.   (There is a large vote.)   Those opposed to
filling the blank with the words 'thirty cents' will say
'no'.   (There is a small vote.)   The ayes have it and
the motion is carried.   The question is now on the
adoption of the amendment to Article I, to strike out
the words 'twenty-five cents' and insert the words
'thirty cents.' As many as favor the adoption of the
amendment will say 'aye.' (There is a large vote.)
Those opposed to the adoption of the amendment will
say 'no.' (No one speaks.)   The ayes have it and the
amendment is adopted."

(The secretary continues to read the by-laws article
by article and section by section and after each section
the chair invites discussion.   When all the by-laws have
been read, the chair speaks.)

The Chair: "The by-laws are now open to amendment
as a whole.   Is there any discussion? (No one speaks.)
As many as favor the adoption of the by-laws as
amended will stand until counted.   (The chairman
pauses for the count.)   Those opposed to the adoption
of the by-laws as amended will stand until counted.
(The chairman pauses for the count.)   There being
thirty-five ayes and three noes, the motion has carried
and the by-laws are adopted."

Tom Barnes (obtaining recognition): "I move that the chair appoint a nominating committee."

George McNeil: "I second the motion."

The Chair: "It has been moved and seconded that the chair appoint a nominating committee. As many as favor the motion will say 'aye.' (There is a large vote.) Those opposed will say 'no.' (There is a small vote.) The motion has carried. Of how many members shall the committee be composed?"

Will Prince (obtaining recognition): "I move that the committee be composed of five members."

Bill Daniel: "I second the motion."

The Chair: "It has been moved and seconded that the committee be composed of five members. As many as favor the motion will say 'aye.' (There is a large vote.) Those opposed will say 'no.' (No one speaks.) The motion has carried and the chair appoints Ben Rice, Vera Sherman, Ralph Myer, Ethel Pierce, and Tom Barnes."

Betty Abbott (obtaining recognition): "I move that we adjourn until two o'clock p. m. Tuesday, April 13, 19—."

Nina Raymond: "I second the motion."

The Chair: "It has been moved and seconded that the club adjourn until two o'clock p. m. Tuesday, April 13, 19—. As many as favor the motion will say 'aye.' (There is a large vote.) Those opposed will say 'no.' (There is a small vote.) The motion has carried and the club stands adjourned until two o'clock p. m. Tuesday, April 13, 19—."

DISCUSSION OF PROCEDURE

Miss Woods: "In the organization meeting Friday we adopted our constitution and by-laws. In the meeting tomorrow after the election of officers we shall be ready to transact business as an organized society. If you do not understand fully how elections are held, please ask questions."

Jane Lee: "Miss Woods, how many names will the nominating committee suggest for each office?"

Miss Woods: "Only one name for each office unless otherwise provided."

Robert Rust: "But suppose we do not want to elect the persons nominated by the nominating committee. What can we do about it?"

Miss Woods: "Nominations from the floor have the same value as nominations made by a nominating committee. Opportunity for nominations from the floor will be given before voting begins."

Floyd Allen: "I do not understand the motion for the previous question. Why is it used?"

Miss Woods: "When the friends or the enemies of a motion wish to have the assembly vote on the motion without further debate they 'move the previous question'; which means they move to have the chair put the question to a vote at once. What vote is required for the previous question?"

Tom Barnes: "A two-thirds vote."

Miss Woods: "That is correct. Why is a two-thirds vote required?"

Vera Sherman: "It is almost like suspending a rule."

Miss Woods: "Yes, that is the reason. Do not forget

that after two-thirds of the members present have voted 'aye' on the previous question the question itself must be put to a vote. Members may vote 'aye' on the previous question and then vote 'no' on the question itself. In other words, the motion for the previous question may be used by the enemies of a motion to bring it to a vote without further debate. The friends of a motion may move the previous question on it so that amendments decreasing its power will not be made.

"What other motion can be made by enemies of a proposition to remove it from consideration without having it go through the usual procedure of debate and vote on adoption?"

Jean Dallas: "They can object to the consideration of the question."

Miss Woods: "Yes, immediately after the proposition is introduced the objection can be made. This motion is made so that the assembly will not waste time on something it does not wish to consider. The objection requires a two-thirds vote.

"What other motion can be made by enemies of a question to keep it from coming to a vote?"

Agnes Sanders: "Postpone indefinitely."

Miss Woods: "Yes, that motion is used to kill a question without risking its coming to a vote. If this motion fails, enemies of the main proposition have time to debate against it or to amend it before it is voted on. A majority vote is sufficient to adopt the motion to postpone indefinitely."

Ben Rice: "The enemies of a proposition may move to lay it on the table, may they not?"

Miss Woods: "They may, but if they wish to kill the proposition that is the wrong motion to use. While a majority can move to lay a motion on the table, a majority can also take it from the table later. The enemies of a motion should remember that at some other meeting those in favor of the motion may be in the majority and thus able to take it from the table and adopt it.

Bertha Jones: "I want to know why it takes a two-thirds vote to postpone a proposition and have it made a special order when it takes only a majority to postpone it and let it be a general order."

Miss Woods: "First you must understand what general and special orders are. Open your textbook at section 112, p. 143. Note that when you make a proposition a special order you, in effect, suspend the rule concerning order of business. Thus a two-thirds vote is required.

"Before the next meeting of the Green Lantern Players I want you to check each of the subsidiary motions. Be certain that you understand how each is used and why. Then test yourself on the privileged and the incidental motions. When are they in order? What form do you use in making each?"

THE SECOND ADJOURNED MEETING

(In room 19 with Leon Camp, temporary chairman, in the chair.)

The Chair: "The meeting will please come to order. The secretary will call the roll. (Everybody is present.) The secretary will read the minutes of the last meeting."

(The minutes are read and approved.)

Chairman of nominating committee (obtaining recognition*):

"Mr. Chairman:

"The committee on nominations appointed by you to nominate the permanent officers for the Green Lantern Players begs leave to report as follows:

We nominate:

George McNeil for president

Nina Raymond for vice-president

Betty Abbott for secretary

David Fox for treasurer

Miss Woods for parliamentarian.

Tom Barnes, Chairman."

The Chair: "You have heard the report of the committee on nominations. It is now in order to make additional nominations for any or all of the offices to be filled."

Nell Talley (o. r.): "I nominate Margaret Richards for vice-president."

Lucy Beard: "I second the nomination."

The Chair: "Are there any further nominations? (No one speaks.) If not, the chair will appoint Bob Hunter, Alice Felton and Jim Wells as tellers to pass paper and pencils to the members. The voting will be by ballot. The first office to be filled is that of president. The committee has nominated George McNeil for this place, but the members are privileged to write on their ballots the name of anyone they wish. As soon as the ballots are completed the tellers will please collect them

*For the remainder of this chapter "obtaining recognition" will be represented by the initials "o. r."

and report to the chair the result. (There is a pause for completion of ballots and tally of tellers.) There being forty votes for George McNeil for president, he is unanimously elected.

"The next office to be filled is that of vice-president. There are two candidates, Nina Raymond and Margaret Richards. (There is a pause for tellers to distribute and collect ballots and make tally.) Margaret Richards has received eight votes and Nina Raymond, thirty-two. Nina Raymond is elected vice-president.

"Next is the office of secretary. The committee has nominated Betty Abbott. (There is a pause while tellers distribute and collect ballots and make tally.) Betty Abbott has received thirty-eight votes, Jane Lee, one, and Agnes Sanders, one. Betty Abbott is elected secretary.

"The committee nomination for treasurer is David Fox. (There is a pause for tellers to distribute and collect ballots and make tally.) David Fox has thirty-nine votes and is elected treasurer.

"The last office is that of parliamentarian. The committee has nominated Miss Woods for that office. (There is a pause for tellers to distribute and collect ballots and make tally.) Miss Woods has received forty votes and is unanimously elected parliamentarian. Will the president now take the chair." (The president now takes the chair and becomes "Mr. Chairman.")

The Chair: "Will the other permanent officers please come to the platform." (These officers are seated.)

The Chair: "What is the pleasure of the club?"

Robert Rust (o. r.): "I wish to offer the following resolution:

"Resolved: That the casting committee be composed of five members chosen by the chair."

Lucy Beard: "I second the resolution."

The Chair: "It has been moved and seconded that the casting committee be composed of five members chosen by the chair. Is there any discussion?"

Grover Thomas: "I object to the consideration of this question."

The Chair: "The consideration of the question has been objected to. Will the assembly consider it? As many as favor the consideration of the question will rise and stand until counted. (There is a pause for the count.) Those opposed will stand until counted. (There is a pause for the count.) There being eighteen ayes and twenty-one noes, the objection fails, since a two-thirds negative vote is required. The resolution that the casting committee be composed of five members chosen by the chair is before the house. Is there any discussion?"

Joe Lucas (o. r.): "We are going to have a director and I should think he would know more about casting than the members of the club."

Carrie Adkins (o. r.): "I think a casting committee of the members would be better because they know the members of the club and would know what parts they could play best. We have worked together in school plays and know what each one can do."

Leon Camp (o. r.): "I move that the resolution be postponed indefinitely."

Bertha Jones: "I second the motion."

The Chair: "It has been moved and seconded that the

resolution that the casting committee be composed of five members chosen by the chair be postponed indefinitely. Is there any discussion?"

Martin West (o. r.): "I move that the resolution be referred to a special committee appointed by the chair."

Sam Hall: "I second the motion."

The Chair: "It has been moved and seconded that the resolution be referred to a special committee appointed by the chair. Is there any discussion?"

Harry Fisher: "A point of order, Mr. President."

The Chair: "State your point of order."

Harry Fisher: "The motion to postpone indefinitely has been made and no action has been taken on it, and the chair has permitted a motion to commit to be made. My point of order is that the motion to commit is not in order."

The Chair: "There are six subsidiary motions which may be applied to a resolution for the purpose of disposing of it. Each of these motions has a certain rank. The motion to postpone indefinitely is sixth and last in rank of these motions; the motion to commit is fourth in rank, so the motion to commit takes precedence of the motion to postpone indefinitely. When a motion is pending, another motion cannot be made unless it is of higher rank than the pending one. Therefore the chair respectfully overrules the point of order."

Jean Dallas (o. r.): "I do not see the use of referring such a question to a committee. It seems to me we could decide that without taking so much time."

The Chair: "Is there any further discussion? (The president pauses.) The question is on the motion to commit. As many as favor referring the proposition to a special committee appointed by the chair will say 'aye.' (There is a small vote.) Those opposed to referring the proposition to a committee will say 'no.' (There is a large vote.) The noes have it and the motion fails."

The Chair: "The question is now on the motion to postpone indefinitely the resolution that the casting committee be composed of five members chosen by the chair. Is there any discussion? (No one speaks.) As many as favor the motion to postpone indefinitely will say 'aye.' (There is a large vote.) Those opposed will say 'no.' (There is a small vote.) The ayes have it and the motion to postpone indefinitely is carried."

The Chair: "According to our by-laws, the club is to have three standing committees, a committee on selection of plays, a committee on finance, and a committee on membership. On the committee on selection of plays, the chair appoints the following: Clarence Kelley, Bertha Jones and Nina Raymond, vice-president, who, according to the by-laws, will act as chairman. On the finance committee, Ralph Myer, John Rogers and Jean Dallas are appointed. The chair appoints on the membership committee, Carrie Adkins, Mary Randall and Bob Hunter."

The Chair: "What is the pleasure of the club?"

Vera Sherman (o. r.): "I move that the director be selected from the Little Theatre staff."

Jane Lee: "I second the motion."

The Chair: "It has been moved and seconded that the

director be selected from the Little Theatre staff. Is there any discussion?"

Ralph Myer (o. r.) : "I move that the consideration of this question be postponed until next Thursday at two p. m."

(The chair confers with the parliamentarian.)

The Chair: "It is not in order to postpone a proposition to a time when no provision has been made for a meeting at that particular time. The proper procedure is to provide for the meeting and then move to postpone the proposition to the specified meeting."

Bob Hunter (o. r.) : "I move that when we adjourn today we adjourn until next Thursday at one o'clock p. m."

Vera Martin: "I second the motion."

The Chair: "It has been moved and seconded that when we adjourn today we adjourn until next Thursday at one o'clock p. m. As many as favor the motion will say 'aye.' (There is a large vote.) Those opposed will say 'no.' (There is a small vote.) The ayes have it and the motion is adopted. The question interrupted by the privileged motion to fix the time to which to adjourn is again before the organization."

Ralph Myer (o. r.) : "I move that the consideration of this question be postponed until next Thursday at two o'clock p. m."

Ethel Pierce: "I second the motion."

The Chair: "It has been moved and seconded to postpone consideration of the motion that the director be selected from the Little Theatre staff until next Thursday at two o'clock p. m. Is there any discussion?"

Will Prince (o. r.): "I move that the motion be amended by adding the words 'and that it be made a special order for two o'clock p. m.' "

Joe Lucas: "I second the motion."

The Chair: "The question is on the amendment of the motion to postpone, to make it a special order for two o'clock p. m. As many as favor the motion to amend will say 'aye.' (There is a large vote.) Those opposed will say 'no.' (There is a small vote.) The ayes have it and the motion to amend is adopted."

Bill Daniel (o. r.): "I move that we reconsider the vote on the amendment which would set the pending question as a special order for two p. m. Thursday."

Jean Dallas: "I second the motion."

The Chair: "The question is on the motion to reconsider the amendment which would set the pending question as a special order for Thursday for two p. m."

Agnes Sanders: "Mr. Chairman."

The Chair: "For what purpose do you wish recognition?"

Agnes: "To discuss the matter of reconsideration."

The Chair: (After conferring with the parliamentarian) "Debate is not in order on a motion to reconsider an undebatable question."

Bob Hunter: "Parliamentary inquiry, Mr. Chairman."

The Chair: "State your parliamentary inquiry."

Bob Hunter: "I thought that an amendment to a motion to postpone to a certain time which would set the proposition as a special order was a debatable question."

The Chair: "The setting of a special order is debatable only when the proposition concerned is not before the assembly. In other words, of the three methods of setting a special order (incidental main motion, incidental motion, and amendment to a motion to postpone to a certain time) only one motion is debatable, the incidental main motion. The motion in question is an amendment to the motion to postpone to a certain time a pending proposition; therefore it is undebatable.

"As many as favor reconsidering the vote by which the amendment was adopted making the question a special order will say 'aye'. (There is a large vote.) Those opposed to reconsidering the vote will say 'no'. (There is a small vote.) The ayes have it and the motion to reconsider the vote by which the amendment was adopted is carried.

"The question now before the house is the adoption of the amendment to the motion to postpone which would set the pending question as a special order for Thursday at two o'clock p. m. As many as favor the adoption of the motion will say 'aye'. (There is a small vote.) Those opposed will say 'no'. (There is a large vote.) The noes have it and the amendment is lost.

"The question now before the house is the motion to postpone until next Thursday at two o'clock p. m. the motion that the director be selected from the Little Theatre staff. Is there any discussion? (No one speaks.) Those in favor of postponing this motion until next Thursday at two o'clock will say 'aye'. (There is a small vote.) Those opposed to postponing this motion will say 'no'. (There is a large vote.) The noes have it and the motion is lost.

"The question now before the house is the motion that the director be selected from the Little Theatre staff. Is there any discussion?"

Will Prince (o. r.): "I move to lay the motion on the table."

Agnes Sanders: "I second the motion."

The Chair: "It has been moved and seconded to table the motion that the director be selected from the Little Theatre staff. Those in favor of the motion to lay on the table will say 'aye'. (There is a large vote.) Those opposed to the motion to lay on the table will say 'no'. (There is a small vote.) The ayes have it and the motion that the director be selected from the Little Theatre staff is laid on the table.

"If there is no further business to come before the club a motion to adjourn is in order."

Bill Daniel (o. r.): "I move that the club adjourn."

Jean Dallas: "I second the motion."

The Chair: "It has been moved and seconded that the club adjourn. As many as favor the motion will say 'aye.' (There is a large vote.) Those opposed will say 'no.' (No one speaks.) The motion carries and the club stands adjourned."

PRESIDENT ROOSEVELT ADDRESSING THE SEVENTY-FOURTH CONGRESS   Copyright by Harris & Ewing

CHAPTER III.

TYPES OF ORGANIZATIONS

TEMPORARY ORGANIZATIONS

1. **Temporary or Mass Meeting.** There are two kinds of organizations—permanent and temporary. A temporary organization is one called to consider some question, or one that is called to take the first steps toward the formation of a permanent organization. A temporary organization is usually known as a mass meeting. Such a meeting is brought about by a public call or by private invitation. Those who are present at a mass meeting are the duly constituted members.

2. **Election of Chairman.** A few minutes after the hour appointed for the meeting, some one rises to his feet, addresses the group and says, "The meeting will please come to order. I move that Mr. A. be elected as chairman of this meeting."

Another person will say, "I second the motion." As many nominations may be made as desired unless a motion to close nominations is made and adopted. A motion to close nominations requires a two-thirds vote for adoption. Nominations are voted in the order that they are made. When one nominee receives a majority of all votes cast he is elected.

The person putting the question states it in this manner: "As many as favor the election of Mr. A. as chairman will say 'aye.'" When the affirmative vote is taken, the question is completed by putting the negative. The results are declared according to the manner of voting. If Mr. A. is not elected, the other nominations are voted on in the order they are made until a chairman is elected.

Very often, if the meeting is called for a specific purpose, the people interested in the meeting will arrange for some one to take the chair. This person calls the meeting to order, then calls for nominations for chairman. After a chairman is elected in the manner set out above (that is, nomination, second, and affirmative majority vote) he is escorted to the platform where he takes the gavel. He may or may not make a short speech, stating the purpose of the meeting, before he proceeds with the business that is to follow.

This question is often asked: "By what authority is a temporary meeting governed?"

A temporary meeting is governed by the authority of the chairman if no other authority is provided. The best method is for the organization to vote that some particular set of rules on parliamentary law be made the rules of the organization.

3. **Election of Secretary.** After a chairman is elected and takes the chair, the first business of the meeting is the election of a secretary. This is done in the same manner in which the chairman was elected, that is, nomination, second, and affirmative majority vote.

The elected secretary comes to the platform, takes a

seat near the chairman, records the minutes of the meeting, and is generally helpful to the chairman and to the successful conduct of the meeting.

4. **Resolutions.** After the secretary is elected the chairman announces that the meeting is ready to consider the purpose for which the meeting was called. He says: "What is the will of the assembly?"

Often the people who had a part in calling the meeting will have a set of resolutions prepared and ready to offer from the floor for the consideration of the group, or some one will rise and move that a committee on resolutions be appointed.

5. **Resolutions from the Floor.** If the resolutions are to be offered from the floor, the person who has them will rise and say:

Member: "Mr. Chairman, this is Mr. Smith speaking."

Chair: "Mr. Smith."

Member: "I offer the following resolution."

The member may either read the resolution himself or send it to the secretary who will read it. After the resolution has been read, a second is in order.

The chairman receives the resolution after it has been seconded and states the question in this manner: "The question is on the adoption of the resolution. (He states the subject matter of the resolution.)"

The chairman waits a short time for some one to rise and seek recognition for the purpose of discussing the resolution. The chairman should try to recognize speakers on the alternate plan, that is, one for the resolution and one against until all have been heard who wish to be heard, or the previous question is ordered. If no one wishes to be heard on the question, the chairman says: "As many as favor the adoption of the resolution will say 'aye.'"

After the affirmative vote is had, he will put the negative by saying: "As many as are opposed to the adoption of this resolution will say 'no.'"

He will then announce the result of the vote: "The ayes have it, and the resolution is adopted;" or "There being forty-seven ayes and twenty noes, the resolution is adopted."

If the resolution is rejected, he will say: "The noes have it; the resolution is lost;" or, "There being twenty ayes and forty-seven noes, the resolution is lost."

6. **Committee on Resolutions.** If the resolutions are to be drawn up by a committee, a motion is made from the floor that the chairman appoint a committee of five or seven to draft resolutions setting out the purpose of the meeting and stating the will of the group and return the resolutions to the assembly for consideration.

7. **Report of Committees.** When the committee on resolutions has returned to the assembly hall, the chairman of the committee rises as soon as the pending business is disposed of, addresses the presiding officer and after being recognized by him advises that the committee is ready to report. Then the chair instructs him to read the report.

If the report made by the committee contains more

than one separate proposition calling for legislative action, the resolutions, propositions or recommendations shall come before the assembly for separate consideration.

The committee's report should read:

"Mr. Chairman:

The committee on resolutions begs leave to report the following resolutions:

(Name)
_____

Chairman of committee."

The resolutions and suggestions should be listed separately and the assembly should take action on them separately. In this way the assembly is not forced to adopt or reject a report or committee recommendations as a whole.

After the chairman of the committee has read his report and the resolutions attached to it, the various resolutions included in the committee's report are put before the assembly. They come before the assembly in the order of their presentation by the committee. As each resolution is read, its adoption moved and seconded, stated by the chair, discussed by the assembly, and voted upon by the assembly, it is either adopted or rejected independently of the report. Thus each resolution reported back to an assembly may be discussed, amended, affirmed, or rejected without affecting any other item in the report. (See Section 81, p. 126-7.)

8. **Adjournment.** When the assembly has finished considering the report of the committee on resolutions and any further business that may have come before

the meeting, the chair asks the secretary to read the minutes of the meeting.* After the minutes have been read and any correction which was needed has been made, the minutes are approved. Then a motion to adjourn is in order. The adjournment of a temporary organization such as the one set forth here is an adjournment *sine die*, unless an adjourned meeting is provided.

9. Order of Business in a Temporary Meeting.

(1) Call to order

(2) Election of a chairman

(3) Election of a secretary

(4) Object of meeting stated by chairman

(5) Motion to appoint a committee on resolutions or other appropriate committee**

(6) Report of the committee

(7) Action by the assembly

(8) Other business

(9) Reading and approval of the minutes of the present meeting

(10) Adjournment

PERMANENT SOCIETIES

10. Organization of Permanent Societies.

Societies become permanent when they adopt a constitution and by-laws and elect permanent officers. They are organ-

---

*In the usual order of business the minutes are read immediately after Roll Call and Excuses for Absent Members, but, since in a temporary meeting adjournment is *sine die*, unless an adjourned meeting has been provided, the minutes must be read at the close of business, just before adjournment.

**A resolution may be offered from the floor and be considered by the assembly without being referred to a committee, if no committee has been selected.

ized by a procedure similar to that of temporary organizations. Those asked to take part in the meetings that will eventually form a permanent organization should be persons who are interested in the principle or accomplishment for which the organization is being formed.

11. **First Meeting.** The time, the place, and the purpose of the meeting should be made known to the persons asked to attend.

A temporary chairman and a temporary secretary are elected. The chairman or some one asked by him to do so should state the purpose of the meeting and invite discussion by those present.

After the discussion has been general, some one rises, addresses the chair, and introduces a resolution that an organization be formed for the purpose stated in the discussion. After the motion has been seconded, stated by the chair, and discussed, it is put to a vote. If it is adopted, a motion is in order that the chairman appoint a committee of five to draft a constitution and by-laws. If this motion is adopted, the chairman appoints a committee on constitution and by-laws. If there is no other business to come before the assembly, a motion to adjourn to a certain time is in order.

12. **Second Meeting.** At the second meeting the temporary chairman calls the meeting to order by saying, "Will the meeting please come to order?"

The secretary then reads the minutes and if there are no corrections they are approved, or if there are corrections they are corrected by an affirmative majority vote.

If the committee on constitution and by-laws is ready

to report, the chairman of the committee addresses the presiding officer by saying, "Mr. Chairman," and upon being recognized by the chair, continues, "The committee on constitution and by-laws is ready to report."

He then reads his report which should be as follows: "Mr. Chairman:

The committee on constitution and by-laws appointed by you begs leave to submit the following constitution and recommends its adoption:

(Name)
_____
Chairman."

13. Adoption of Constitution. The entire constitution is read throughout. A motion is then in order to adopt the constitution. If the motion is seconded, and stated by the chair, the correct procedure is as follows: It is read again, section by section, and paragraph by paragraph. After each paragraph is read, the chair should call for discussion, explanations, and amendments, and then pass on to the next paragraph. After the constitution has been amended paragraph by paragraph, it is open to amendment as a whole. Amendments to the constitution before adoption require a majority vote only.

After there has been time to amend and discuss the constitution as a whole, the chair asks the assembly if it is ready for the question. If it is ready the chair puts the question, and the constitution is adopted or rejected. In some organizations the members sign the constitution and pay a fee. After the constitution has been adopted, it is then in order that some one move the adoption of the by-laws.

The consideration and adoption of the by-laws is treated in the same manner as the constitution.

14. **Nominating Committee.** The constitution and by-laws having been adopted, the next order of business is the election of the permanent officers of the organization. A motion is in order that a nominating committee of three be appointed by the chairman to nominate the permanent officers of the organization as provided in the constitution.

When the nominating committee is ready to report, the chairman of the committee should address the chair, receive recognition and read the report of the committee.

15. **Election of Officers.** After the chairman of the nominating committee has read the nominations made by the committee the chair should inquire if there are further nominations. A member may nominate one person for one of the offices or may propose an entirely new ticket, that is, one person for every office to be filled. If no further nominations are made and no motion to close nominations is made the chair should inquire if there are further nominations before he proceeds with the election. Inasmuch as the constitution or by-laws usually provide that election shall be by ballot, the chair appoints tellers to distribute the ballots for each election.

The organization may provide a ballot which contains the names of all nominees offered by the nominating committee with blanks left for all additional nominations which may be made from the floor or by the individual members as they vote. In the event the organization selects this way of balloting, the chairman should ask for additional nominations for all offices before the ballots are distributed.

After all of the officers have been elected, the permanent organization is complete.

DELEGATE BODIES

16. Temporary Organization of Delegate Bodies. Delegates represent groups which belong to a permanent organization. A meeting of delegates forms a temporary organization and then a permanent organization, performs the duties for which it has met, and adjourns *sine die*.

17. Committee on Credentials. After the temporary chairman and secretary have been elected, it is in order to move that a committee on credentials be appointed to inspect the credentials of the delegates and to determine who are the eligible ones. Some one should address the chair and after receiving recognition should say: "I move that a committee of five be appointed by the chair to examine the credentials of the delegates and report back to the meeting."

If the motion calls simply for the selection of a credentials committee the chairman may proceed as in section 65, p. 116 to determine the number of the committeemen, and the way in which they are to be selected. All other committees, needed in such a meeting, must be appointed or elected on a motion that such committees be formed. In delegate bodies committees are usually appointed to consider such questions as platform and resolutions, canvassing election returns, ways and means, nominations and elections, credentials, and permanent organization.

18. **Voting on Credentials.** After the committee on credentials has met and considered the credentials, it should report back to the organization the names of those delegates having proper credentials, and the names of those having doubtful or contested ones. It should also offer recommendations as to the disposition of the contested or doubtful credentials. The organization may adopt or reject these recommendations.

In voting on the credentials in dispute, only those delegates whose credentials are undisputed can vote.

19. **Selection of Permanent Officers and Committees.** The next order of business is the election of permanent officers. After the committee on permanent organization has made its report the chairman may inquire if there are further nominations for permanent officers from the floor. (Section 15, p. 87.)

After the permanent officers have been elected, the temporary officers turn the meeting over to them, and the business of the convention may proceed.

Committees should be either appointed by the chair or elected by the members, according to the custom of the group. Such committees as are needed for the successful conduct of the meeting should be formed, for example: committee on platform and resolutions, committee on nominations, committee on organization, and others. While these committees are at work, the convention may consider other business or hear the views of different persons.

When a meeting of this type has completed its labors, it adjourns *sine die*, however, it may adjourn or recess from day to day until it has finished.

20. **Order of Business for Conventions or Delegate Bodies.**

    (1) Call to order
    (2) Election of temporary chairman
    (3) Election of temporary secretary
    (4) Appointment of committees: credentials, organization, platform and resolutions, and others
    (5) Recess or informal proceedings
    (6) Report of committee on credentials
    (7) Action on findings of committee
    (8) Report of committee on permanent organization*
    (9) Election of permanent officers
    (10) Installation of permanent officers
    (11) Appointment of other committees
    (12) Communications, petitions, memorials
    (13) Report of committees
        a. Platform and resolutions
        b. Ways and means
        c. Nominations and elections
        d. Canvassing election returns
    (14) Other business
    (15) Reading and approval of minutes
    (16) Adjournment.

---

*In delegate bodies the committee on permanent organization performs the duties of a nominating committee.

STUDY AND DISCUSSION TOPICS

1. What is the difference between the method of calling a mass meeting and the method of calling a meeting for the purpose of forming a permanent organization?

2. What is the difference in purpose of the two meetings?

3. Name in order the steps to be followed in forming a temporary organization; a permanent society.

4. What kind of assemblies are called delegate bodies?

5. Which of the three types of organizations would be best to carry out the purpose of each of the following groups?

Group of boys wishing to organize a debating society,

Group of citizens wishing to petition the city council for street lights in certain sections of the city,

Meeting of state organization of Garden Clubs.

6. When are minutes read in a temporary or mass meeting?

7. On whom does the obligation for leadership in a mass or temporary meeting fall?

8. What is the significance of the committee on credentials?

CHAPTER IV.

ORGANIC LAW AND OFFICERS

ORGANIC LAW

21. **Definition.** These four classes of rules or regulations provide for the government of organizations, such as the transaction of business, the election of officers, and all other important matters.

Many organizations have all four types of rules. Others may have but one or two.

CONSTITUTION

22. **What It Should Contain.** The constitution should be as brief as possible. It should contain nothing that can be suspended. It should be dated as of the day of adoption and should be signed by the persons taking part in the organization. The number of ayes and noes should be recorded on the constitution itself.

A model constitution should contain such points as:

    (1) Name
    (2) Object

(3) Qualifications for membership

(4) Officers and manner of electing

(5) What constitutes a quorum

(6) Number and day of meetings

(7) Nominating committee

(8) Parliamentary law authority

(9) Provision for amendments.

The method of adopting a constitution is found in section 13, p. 86 on permanent organization.

23. Amendments to the Constitution. The constitution should provide that an amendment to it be submitted in writing at a regular meeting before the time it is to be considered for adoption, and that the adoption of the amendment require a two-thirds vote of the members present. (See Section 180, p. 191.)

When a constitution does not provide for its own amendment, it may be amended at any regular meeting of the organization by a majority vote of all the members.

However, if the proposed amendment is submitted in writing at the previous regular meeting, it may be adopted by a two-thirds vote of the members voting, a quorum being present.

Amendments to the constitution go into effect at the time of their adoption unless the organization decides otherwise. When the amendment is pending, a motion may be made that the amendment, if adopted, not go into effect until some named date. If this motion is adopted, the amendment, if adopted, will not go into effect until the date named. The adoption of this motion to defer the date of effect requires a majority vote.

When an amendment to the constitution is pending of which notice has been given as required in the constitution, and an amendment to the amendment is offered, it may be considered and adopted by a majority vote without notice. However, no amendment to the pending amendment can be made that increases the modification which the amendment proposes.*

24.   Example of a Constitution.

CONSTITUTION OF THE GEOGRAPHIC SOCIETY OF MULLENTOWN, ARIZONA

Article I.   Name

The name of this organization shall be the Geographic Society.

Article II.   Object

The object of this organization shall be to study the geography of the surrounding country.

Article III.   Membership

Section 1.   Membership in this organization shall be limited to three classes: active, associate, and honorary. The membership of this society shall be composed of persons living within the Harris Mullen Survey.

---

*An amendment to the pending amendment might be offered which would change the rule to any figure between the one in the constitution and the one proposed by the pending amendment.

For example: Notice is given that an amendment to the constitution will be offered changing the monthly dues from twenty-five cents to fifty cents. When this amendment comes up for consideration, an amendment to this amendment is in order changing the dues to any figure between twenty-five cents and fifty cents; but an amount greater than fifty cents or less than twenty-five cents would not be in order.

Section 2. A majority of members of the organization shall elect additional members.

Section 3. Active members shall attend at least one-half of the regular meetings and be responsible for the program of study adopted by the organization.

Section 4. Associate members shall be entitled to all the privileges of the club except those of voting and holding office; however, they shall not be held responsible for the program of study.

Section 5. Honorary members are those who are given membership in the organization for some worthy service in the field which the society studies. They shall be elected by the unanimous vote of the organization.

Article IV. Officers

Section 1. The officers of this organization shall be a president, a vice-president, a secretary, and a treasurer.

Section 2. All officers of this organization shall be elected by ballot at the annual meeting and shall hold office until the next annual election, or until their successors are elected.

Section 3. A majority of all votes cast shall be necessary for an election.

Section 4. Vacancies in office shall be filled by special election.

Article V. Quorum

One-third of the active membership of the society shall be necessary for a quorum.

Article VI. Meetings

Section 1. The annual meeting of the society shall be held on the third Monday in May.

Section 2. Regular meetings shall be held on the first Monday of each month.

Section 3. Special meetings shall be called by the president or the vice-president in the absence of the president, or by any five members of the society.

Article VII. Nominating Committee

The nominating committee shall be appointed by the president, not later than the first Monday in April. It shall consist of five members of the organization.

Article VIII. Authority in Parliamentary Law

This organization shall be governed by rules of parliamentary law, as found in "Mr. Chairman," by Oveta Culp Hobby.

Article IX. Amendments

This constitution may be amended at any regular meeting; provided, that the amendment shall have been submitted at the last regular meeting in writing, and that the adoption of the amendment shall require a two-thirds vote of the members present.

BY-LAWS

25. **What They Contain.** The by-laws contain fundamental rules that are not in the constitution. They are usually given in more detail than are provisions in the constitution. They govern such matters as:

Amount of dues
Duties of officers
Order of business
Names and duties of committees
Time and place of meeting
Provision for their own amendment and suspension.

If the by-laws contain rules that the organization may ever wish to suspend, provision for suspension should be made a part of the by-laws. By-laws require a two-thirds vote for their suspension or their amendment. (See Section 180, p. 191.)

26. **An Example of By-laws.**

BY-LAWS OF THE GEOGRAPHIC SOCIETY OF MULLENTOWN

Article I. Dues

The dues of the Geographic Society shall be one dollar per year, payable at the annual meeting for the year succeeding.

Article II. Duties of the Officers

Section 1. The president shall preside at all meetings when he is present. He shall appoint all committees, standing and special. He shall supervise the program of study.

Section 2. The vice-president shall preside at the meetings in the absence of the president. He shall be chairman of the committee on program.

Section 3. The secretary shall keep an accurate record of the meetings, attend to all correspondence given him, take care of all materials to be used by committees, keep an up-to-date membership list, and keep a record of the attendance.

Section 4.   The treasurer shall keep a faithful account of all receipts and disbursements.   He shall report annually to the organization.   He shall keep his books up to date and be ready to report at any time he may be called upon by the president.

Article III.   Committees

Section 1.   There shall be four standing committees:

>   Committee on program
>   Committee on finance
>   Committee on house
>   Committee on membership.

Section 2.   The committee on program shall present to the club a program of study for each coming year and be responsible for its development.

Section 3.   The committee on finance shall attend to all matters regarding money and shall report to the organization at the annual meeting, or when called upon by the president.

Section 4.   The committee on house shall be responsible for the meeting place and all other arrangements as to housing, janitors, lighting, etc.

Section 5.   The committee on membership shall vouch for all new persons who are offered for membership.

Article IV.   Meetings

The regular meeting of the organization shall be held at four o'clock p. m. on the first Monday in each month.

Article V.   Order   of   Business

1. Call to order
2. Roll call
3. Excuses for absent members
4. Reading of the minutes
5. Report of the treasurer
6. Reports of standing committees
7. Reports of special committees
8. Unfinished business
9. New business
10. Program for the day
11. Adjournment.

Article VI.   Suspension

The suspension of any part of these by-laws shall require a two-thirds vote.

Article VII.   Amendment

These by-laws may be amended at any regular meeting if notice of the proposed amendments has been given. A two-thirds vote of the members present shall be required for the adoption of the amendments.

RULES OF ORDER

27. **Definition.** These are rules governing the orderly transaction of business and relating to the policy of the organization. Often an organization will make the by-laws serve the purpose of the rules of order or make the rules of order take the place of the by-laws. A rule of order before adoption is a main motion and may be amended by a majority vote. A majority vote is necessary to adopt a rule of order. After a rule of order

has been adopted, if it is to be amended, notice must be given of the proposed amendments, and the vote on adoption be a two-thirds vote of the members present.

A rule of order can be suspended by a two-thirds vote. The purpose for which the suspension was obtained must be stated and the suspension is available for the named purpose only. It is well to remember that no rule requiring previous notice and a two-thirds vote for its amendment can be suspended by a vote of less than two-thirds of the members present. Example of a rule of order:

"*Resolved*, That the Geographic Society will not consider matters that will lead to disputes or quarrels."

STANDING RULES

28. **Definition.** Standing rules are rarely adopted as a group. They are more often adopted as the need for them arises. They relate largely to matters of policy which may change as the situation changes, such as meeting place and types of programs. These rules are of such nature that they can be introduced, considered, and adopted without previous notice. They require only a majority vote. They can be suspended by a majority vote or they can be amended or rescinded without notice by a two-thirds vote. If notice has been given, a majority vote is sufficient. The vote on adoption of these rules may be reconsidered. Likewise a vote on their amendment before and after adoption can be reconsidered.

Example of a standing rule:

"*Resolved*, That the Geographic Society meet in the

auditorium of the main library during the summer months."

OFFICERS

29. **In Temporary Organizations.** The presiding officer and the secretary usually are the only officers of a temporary organization. The duties of these officers are much the same as those of officers in a permanent organization.

30. **Permanent Societies.** Permanent societies have a president, one or more vice-presidents, a recording secretary, and a treasurer. Often a corresponding secretary and a parliamentarian are added to the list of officers.

31. **Duties of Officers.** The duties of the executive officers of a permanent organization should be clearly set out in the by-laws of the organization. These duties will vary according to the type of club or society.

32. **Presiding Officer.** The chairman, president, regent, moderator, or other person presiding should:

(1) Call the meeting to order.

(2) Determine the presence of a quorum.

(3) Present the minutes for approval or correction.

(4) Follow the order of business.

(5) Entertain propositions from members.

(6) Determine priority of recognition.

(7) State the questions and put them to a vote.

(8) Declare the results of a vote.

(9) When the order of business is completed, inform the assembly that the calendar is clear.

(10) Decide upon all points of order.

(11) Give his reasons for his decisions on points of order.

(12) Enforce the rules of the assembly.

33. The Chairman in Debate. It is a general principle of parliamentary law that the chairman does not partici- pate in debate, except that he may speak to a point of order or on a question of appeal in preference to anyone else. If he wishes to take part in debate he may do so, but he must call some one else to the chair to preside. He must then seek recognition as would any other mem- ber. He must not resume the chair until the matter upon which he has spoken is no longer before the house.

If the chairman is a member of the assembly, he may vote when his vote would break a tie and he may vote when his vote would cause a tie. He may vote by ballot but his vote must be in the hands of the tellers before any of the votes have been counted. If he votes on a roll call, he votes last.

The chairman may sit while he states a question, but he should stand while he puts the question to a vote.

The presiding officer always refers to himself as "the chair." He never puts a question to a vote that affects himself, but calls someone else to the chair.

If the chairman refuses to announce a vote or conduct the affairs of the meeting along parliamentary lines, the members may declare the chair vacant and elect another presiding officer.

34. Vice-President. The first vice-president will serve as president in the absence of the president. For this reason he should be selected with great care. The number of vice-presidents in an organization will depend upon the character of the organization. The duties of the vice-presidents should be listed in the by-laws.

35. Recording Secretary. The recording secretary should:

(1) Keep the minutes and a record of all proceedings.

(2) Read the minutes and propositions submitted by the members.

(3) Call the roll, if required.

(4) Keep a complete record of all reports, petitions, publicity, and other papers.

(5) Keep an up-to-date copy of the constitution, by-laws, rules of order, and standing rules.

(6) Keep an up-to-date membership list.

(7) Send out all notices required by the organization.

(8) Call the meeting to order in the absence of the president and vice-president and preside until the election of a temporary chairman.

(9) Prepare for the use of the chairman an accurate order of business and a list of all committees, special and standing.

(10) Keep a complete file of all committee reports and matters referred to committees.

(11) Sign all minutes.

36. Minutes. The minutes kept by the secretary should include the following points:

(1) Kind of meeting, regular or special.

(2) Date, hour, and place of meeting.

(3) Person presiding.

(4) Person acting as secretary.

(5) Reading of minutes.

(6) Reports of committees.

(7) Record of the unfinished business discussed and disposition of same.

(8) Record of new business and disposition of same.

(9) Other business or program for the day.

(10) Adjournment.

37. An Example of Minutes.

"The Geographic Society met in regular session at the Odd Fellows' Hall on the first Monday in May at four o'clock p. m.

"Mr. John Evans presided and Mrs. Alice Snowden served as secretary.

"The minutes of the previous meeting were read and with one correction were approved. The correction was that Mrs. Smith made the motion about the change in a meeting-place instead of Mrs. Alexander as the minutes had reported.

"The committee on entertainment reported that it had been able to obtain the assistance of the Historical Society in securing an outside speaker for the schools.

"The committee on program reported that several programs of work had been considered and that the committee would make its report at the next regular meeting.

"The committee on courtesy, a special committee appointed by the president to entertain the guest speaker, reported its activities.

"The resolution which was pending at the time of adjournment at the last meeting of the organization was considered. The resolution was postponed indefinitely on the motion of Mrs. Roberts and the second of Mrs. Henderson. A copy of this resolution is attached and hereby made a part of the minutes.

"Mrs. Roberts introduced a resolution which had for its purpose the combining of the Geographic Society with the Historical Society. Mrs. Smith seconded the adoption of the resolution. After some discussion, Mrs. Fletcher moved that the resolution be referred to the committee of the whole. Mr. Harrison seconded the motion. The motion carried. Mr. Luther moved that the Geographic Society resolve itself into the committee of the whole for the purpose of considering the resolution. Mr. Brown seconded the motion. The motion was adopted, and the organization resolved itself into the committee of the whole. At five o'clock the committee rose and reported its progress to the organization.

"The hour having arrived for the program, the president called the program chairman to the chair. Mrs. Hardy introduced the speaker for the day, who spoke most interestingly on 'Indication of Minerals in Topography.'

"After the program was completed, Mrs. Lovelace moved to adjourn and Mr. Stringer seconded the motion. The motion was adopted."

38. **Corresponding Secretary.** When there is much correspondence to be handled, a corresponding secretary is elected, who answers correspondence according to the wishes of the board of directors or the executive committee.

39. **Treasurer.** As a rule the treasurer acts as the banker for the organization. He receives all funds and

pays them out on the order of the organization. He is expected to keep his books up to date, and to help the board of directors in any way he can. He makes an annual report at the annual meeting, or at any other time he may be asked to do so. If the report is to be audited, the treasurer should see that the information is in the hands of the auditor at the proper time. The treasurer's duties will vary with the type of organization he serves. It is always well to secure the services of a competent bookkeeper when setting up the books.

40. Form of Treasurer's Report.

Receipts for the Year 19—.

Balance on hand January 1, 19—	$170.06
Members' dues	500.00
Donations	100.00
Receipts from benefit lecture	75.00
Total	$845.06

Disbursements for the Year 19—.

Rental	$ 76.00
Janitor	56.00
Tickets and programs	75.00
Gifts	26.00
Stage hands	32.00
Total disbursements	$265.00
Balance on hand December 31, 19—	580.06
Total	$845.06

(Name) ....

Treasurer

Examined and found true and correct.

Smith and Robertson, Auditors.

41. Executive Secretary. The executive secretary of an organization is usually a paid employee whose duties are outlined by the president and the board of directors.

42. Parliamentarian. The duties of parliamentarian vary according to the rules of the body and the technical knowledge of the presiding officer. However, it is the business of the parliamentarian to follow debate closely, list either on paper or in his mind the sequence of the motions, be prepared to advise the chair as to whether or not a certain motion is in order, examine all amendments as they are offered to determine whether or not they are germane, be prepared to answer inquiries from the chairman on points of order, and parliamentary inquiries and to determine questions of privilege. It is safe to say that all procedural matters come within the duties of the Parliamentarian.

43. Obligations of Officers. When an officer is elected and consents to serve, he must discharge the duties of his office to the best of his ability. If a person is elected to an office, appointed on a committee, or appointed to some other duty, he must decline at once if he is present and does not wish to serve. If he declines, the organization fills the place with some other person. If he is not present, he should either accept or reject the appointment as soon as notified. After a person has served as an officer, he cannot dismiss his responsibilities by his resignation. His resignation must be accepted before he is relieved of his duties.

STUDY AND DISCUSSION TOPICS

1. Can you give any good reason for dividing the laws of an organization into three parts—constitution, by-laws, and rules of order?

2. Define—active member; associate member; honorary member.

3. Why is it wise to put small details in by-laws and put only important principles in the constitution?

4. When should the term, "the chair", be used in speaking of the presiding officer? By whom?

5. What are the chief duties of the chairman?

6. May the chair take part in debate? If so, under what circumstances?

7. Why is it important for the minutes to be corrected and approved by the assembly?

8. What are the duties of the parliamentarian?

9. What is the reason for providing that amendments to the constitution must be submitted in writing at a regular meeting of an organization before the meeting at which they are considered?

10. Why do constitutions usually provide that amendments must be adopted by a two-thirds vote?

11. Prepare a set of minutes, using Section 36 as an outline.

CHAPTER V.

COMMITTEES

DEFINITION

44. **Committees Defined.** Committees are small assemblies. They may be thought of as subordinate groups of the parent group for whom they perform some certain duty. Committees are very important parts of an organization. Much work of the parent group is done in committees.

TYPES OF COMMITTEES

45. **Committees Classified.** Committees may be divided into five distinct classes:

(1) Boards of management, which may include boards of directors, boards of trustees, and boards of managers.

(2) Executive councils appointed by such boards of management.

(3) Committee of the whole, a committee belonging to or being a part of every organization, also

quasi-committee of the whole and informal consideration.

(4) Standing committees, which are provided for in the organic law of an organization.

(5) Special committees, which are provided for by resolutions.

46. Boards of Management. The size of a board of management will depend upon the size and type of organization which it represents.

The powers and duties of such boards are provided for in the organic law of the society and by rules adopted by the parent group. These boards usually function from one meeting to the next for organizations that do not meet very often. Members of the board of management are responsible for their committees during the term for which they are appointed. Many constitutions provide that the terms of one-third of the members of the board shall expire every year. At each annual meeting members are elected to fill the vacancies, and officers for the coming year are elected.

Boards of management are usually required to make an annual report to the organization. Propositions are rarely referred to the boards of management. They almost always originate with the board.

47. Executive Councils. The members of the executive council are usually taken from the membership of the board of directors. The executive council acts for the board of management between the meetings of the board. The board in such case delegates its authority to the executive council.

In many organizations the executive council is composed of the president, the vice-president, the secretary, the treasurer, and the parliamentarian of the organization.

48. Committees Permitting Free Debate. There are three ways of permitting free debate on a proposition; they are in the order of their rank:

(1) Committee of the whole.

(2) Quasi-committee of the whole.

(3) Informal consideration of a question.

COMMITTEE OF THE WHOLE

49. Definition. The committee of the whole is the whole organization acting in the form of a committee. This practice is most often used in legislative assemblies. It is possible to consider a proposition more thoroughly in this way than in the regular procedure.

50. Motion to Resolve into Committee of the Whole. When an organization wishes to resolve itself into a committee of the whole, a motion is made that the organization resolve itself into the committee of the whole to consider the matter under discussion. If the motion is adopted, the chairman of the organization calls another member to the chair and becomes a member of the committee, or a chairman may be elected by the committee.

51. Rank of Motion. To commit a proposition to the committee of the whole is debatable as to the propriety of the commitment. The motion has the same status as a motion to commit or refer or re-refer. It takes precedence of a motion to amend and a motion to postpone indefinitely. It yields to any privileged question or to any incidental question. It yields to the motion to lay on the table, the motion for the previous question, or the motion to postpone to a certain day. A motion to go into committee of the whole to consider a question not pending is a main motion and debatable.

52. Procedure in Committee of the Whole. The committee of the whole is governed by the rules of the organization with the exceptions set out herein. The only motions that are in order when an organization is sitting as a committee of the whole are to amend, to adopt, to rise, or to rise and report. The motion to rise in the committee of the whole is the same as the motion to adjourn in the organization. If the committee wishes to adjourn, the motion is usually to the effect that "The committee of the whole rise." Voting by roll call cannot be demanded in the committee of the whole.

An appeal from the decision of the chair can be made, but no person may speak more than once on appeal and it must be voted on directly, as the subsidiary motions to lay on the table and to postpone are not permitted in committee of the whole.

53. Quorum. The same number is necessary for a quorum in the committee of the whole as is necessary in the organization proper. The committee of the whole, when it finds itself without a quorum, asks permission to rise and report its lack of quorum to the organization.

54. Subcommittee Not Permitted. The committee of the whole may not appoint a subcommittee to act for it or to report to the large committee.

55. Questions Not in Order. Questions of privilege

are not in order in the committee of the whole. Debate cannot be limited unless the organization has prescribed such limits before the group resolved itself into the committee of the whole.

No motion for the previous question is in order during the time the committee sits as a whole. Reconsideration is not permissible.

56. Free Debate. In the committee of the whole a member may speak as often as he can get the floor and the time limit is the same as in the assembly proper. Should the organization have limited debate or set the time when the committee should rise, the committee must abide by these regulations. The motion to rise is undebatable and is always in order except when another member has the floor.

57. Minutes. No exact minutes are kept in the committee of the whole, only the memoranda needed by the chairman in making a report to the organization.

58. Chairman. As soon as the committee has risen the chairman resumes the chair and asks for the report of the committee.

The chairman of the committee rises, addresses the chair, and reports the progress made in committee of the whole. If the committee of the whole failed to reach a conclusion, this must be reported. If amendments were adopted in the committee of the whole, the committee chairman will say, "The committee of the whole has had under consideration (here he states the nature of the proposition) and has directed me to report the same with amendments." He then reads the amendment or amendments and the chair puts the question on the amendments as a whole unless some member asks for a separate vote. An amendment on which a separate vote is asked may be debated and amended after being reported from committee of the whole. If no amendments are reported from committee of the whole, the chair immediately puts the question on the proposition which was discussed in committee of the whole.

59. **Disorder.** Should disorder occur in the committee of the whole, the regular chairman or president of the organization may resume the chair and restore order.

QUASI-COMMITTEE OF THE WHOLE

60. **Definition.** Quasi-committee of the whole is a procedure which permits free debate as if in committee of the whole. This form of deliberation is used often in legislative bodies. The form of the motion is: "I move that the proposition be considered as if in committee of the whole." If the motion is adopted, all the rules of free debate in the committee of the whole apply; but the presiding officer of the organization retains the chair. The adoption of any motion other than the one to amend puts an end to the quasi-committee of the whole.

A matter reported by the quasi-committee has the same status as a proposition reported by any other committee.

No minutes are kept in such a meeting, except memoranda necessary for the chairman's report which is written in the minutes.

INFORMAL CONSIDERATION

61. Definition. Informal consideration is the method used to secure free debate in small societies.

Some member moves that the question be considered informally. This motion, if adopted, opens the main question and all amendments to free debate. No member may speak the second time if a member who has not spoken wishes to speak. The motion to consider informally applies only to the main motion and the amendments to the main motion. Other motions fall under the regular rules of debate. Debate may be limited or may be closed by a two-thirds vote when a group is considering a question informally.

All votes taken under an informal consideration are as votes taken in regular meetings. When the question which the group agreed to consider informally is disposed of, the society is again in regular session without any motion or vote.

EX OFFICIO MEMBERS

62. Ex Officio. A person who is an *ex-officio* member of a board or committee is so because of some office or position which he holds. The mayor of a city may be an *ex-officio* member of the board of directors of the art museum, or the governor of the state may be an *ex-officio* member of the board of directors of a state institution. When such a person ceases to hold the office, his membership on the board is at an end. If the *ex-officio* member holds office by the authority of the society, his obligations and privileges are the same as any member of the board or committee. When the *ex-officio* member is not under the authority of the board of directors, such as the mayor of the city or the governor of a state, he has all the privileges, including the right to vote, but none of the obligations of membership.

STANDING AND SPECIAL COMMITTEES

63. Standing Committees. These are usually provided for in the by-laws or rules of order of an organization. Their authority is usually prescribed also. A standing committee is never dissolved unless the authority which created it is amended or repealed. The membership of the committee may change, but the committee itself is continuous.

64. Special Committees. A special committee is one which is appointed for a particular purpose. It has authority to act only on the matter submitted to it. The committee is automatically discharged when it makes its report to the parent group; although it may be revived by a vote and the same matter resubmitted.

65. Standing and Special Committees: Organization and Procedure. How committees are formed: In the event a motion is made and adopted to appoint a committee to consider certain matters, and neither the number of persons to make up the committee nor the method of selecting the membership has been provided, the chair may inquire of the assembly: "How many members shall make up the committee?"

Generally a motion will follow that a certain number make up the committee. Members may propose various numbers without a motion. Each one is treated as a separate proposition. The largest number is put first and so on in the order of their size until some number is agreed upon. (See Section 209 (6), p. 224 and Section 214, p. 228-9.)

After such a motion is adopted in its original form or its amended form, the chair may inquire: "How shall the members of the committee be appointed?"

A motion is then in order that they be:

(1) Appointed by the chair,

(2) Nominated and elected by the assembly, or

(3) Nominated by the chair and elected by the assembly.

If a committee is to be appointed after adjournment, permission must be given by the assembly before adjournment. The chair cannot appoint any committee unless authority is given him by the assembly or by right of some rule of the organization.

66. **Selection of Chairman.** The question often arises as to whether or not the first named person on a committee is the chairman. Authorities are conflicting. The fair position to take is that the first named person is not chairman unless so named by the appointive or elective power.*

In the event a chairman is not so named, the committee selects its own chairman; the first named person calls the

---

*Robert's Rules of Order Revised states:

"Unless the assembly has appointed a chairman, either directly or through its presiding officer, the first named on a committee, and in his absence the next named member, becomes chairman and so on and should act as such unless the committee by a majority of its number elects a chairman, which it has the right to do if the assembly has not appointed one."

This author takes the position that it is better to state a positive rule on this point and avoid misunderstanding.

committee together, and the committee proceeds to elect a chairman.

67. Notification of Members of a Committee. When a committee has been selected, the secretary should prepare a copy of the resolution which created the committee together with a list of the members and give it to the chairman, if one has been named; if one has not been named he should hand the material to the person first named.

68. Size of Committees. Committees appointed to carry out certain instructions should be small and of the same mind. Committees appointed to make certain investigations or to consider material of a controversial nature should be large and composed of persons representing the various schools of thought in the organization.

69. Presiding Officer of a Committee. The committee has a chairman who is appointed by the presiding officer, elected by the parent group, or elected by the committee itself.

70. Duties of the Chairman.

He calls the committee together.

He submits all matters for consideration in their proper order.

The chairman of the committee is often the most active member in discussion.

If the committee is small the chairman may act as secretary; although it is better to have a regular secretary.

If the chairman or vice-chairman fails or refuses to call a meeting, the committee may meet on the call of any two members.

71. Duties of the Secretary. The secretary may be a member of the committee, elected by the committee or an employed person selected by the committee. It is his duty to see that all records of the committee are kept with the strictest accuracy. The secretary is custodian of all papers referred to the committee, as well as all matters that originate in the committee. The secretary keeps the minutes of the committee.

72. Items Included in Committee Minutes.

(1) Kind of meeting, regular or special
(2) Date, hour, and place of meeting
(3) Person presiding
(4) Person acting as secretary
(5) Reading of minutes
(6) Committee report
(7) Record of the unfinished business discussed and disposition
(8) Record of the new business discussed and disposition
(9) Adjournment.

73. An Example of Minutes.

"Minutes of the Finance Committee, May 11, 19—.

"The finance committee met in regular meeting at the library auditorium on the eleventh of May, 19—, at eight o'clock p. m. Mr. John Snowden presided and Miss Emily Lawther served as secretary.

"The minutes of the previous meeting were read and approved.

"The chairman laid the matter of the budget before the committee, it being unfinished business. The subcommittee on the budget reported. The report is attached and made a part of these minutes.

"The committee considered the report of the subcommittee and adopted the following resolutions which are attached to these minutes and made a part of them:

(1) That the finance committee recommend that the Geographic Society do not consider an increase in rental for the meeting place.

(2) That the finance committee recommend to the assembly the employment of an executive secretary.

(3) That the finance committee recommend to the assembly that speakers from this state be given consideration over speakers from more remote points in order to conserve funds set aside for traveling expense.

"The committee then proceeded to make the budget. Mr. Hill moved that the committee recommend the budget to the assembly for adoption. Mr. Wilson seconded the motion. It carried unanimously.

The budget:

Rental	$ 150.00
Speakers' fees	500.00
Traveling expenses	200.00
Decorations	25.00
Janitor	50.00
Advertising	50.00
Tickets and programs	75.00
Secretary	1,200.00
Office expenses	100.00
Other expenses	125.00
Total	$2,475.00

"Mr. Johnson moved that the subcommittee appointed by the committee on finance make an investigation and report concerning suitable housing quarters. Mr. Green seconded the motion. The motion was adopted.

"Mr. Marks introduced a motion to change the date and hour of meeting from eight o'clock p.m. on each second Monday of the month to seven-thirty o'clock p.m. on each third Monday of the month. Mr. Potts seconded the motion. The motion was discussed, but it failed of adoption when put to a vote.

"Mr. Erickson moved that the committee adjourn until eight o'clock p.m. on the second Monday in June. The motion was adopted."

74. Procedure in Committees. The procedure in committees is governed by the same rules that govern parent groups whenever the rules are applicable.

It is the duty of the chairman to call a committee meeting. If the chairman for any reason fails to call a meeting, the vice-chairman may call one. In the event neither the chairman nor the vice-chairman calls a meeting, the committee may meet on the call of any two members.

Committees should hear the views of members of the organization on matters before the committee. However, the committee has a right to go into executive session when the hearings are over and the committee is about to begin deliberations.

The motions to limit or close debate are not permitted in committees, however, and a member may speak as often as he can get the floor. Another notable exception is the motion for reconsideration. A motion for reconsideration can be made at any time in a committee regardless of the lapse of time since the motion sought to be reconsidered was acted upon, provided the matter is still in committee. The motion to reconsider under such circumstances can be made by anyone who did not vote with the minority. It may be made by one who was absent when the vote was taken. The motion to reconsider requires a two-thirds vote. However, if every person who voted on the prevailing side is present when the motion for reconsideration is made, or if ample notice had been given that the reconsideration will be moved, a majority vote is sufficient.

When amendments are pending to a proposition referred to a committee, the amendments must be returned to the organization with the proposition. The committee may recommend their adoption or their rejection, or make no recommendation at all.

Propositions referred to a committee by the parent group take precedence of propositions that the committee itself originates. A committee must not alter the original proposition or any of the pending amendments submitted with it, but should offer its amendments to the proposition or its amendments to the referred amendments on a separate sheet of paper.

When the proposition referred to a committee has a preamble, or an enacting clause, as the case may be, the preamble is always amended last so that the amendments to the text can be included in the preamble. This is true also of propositions which originate in committees.

75. Treatment of Committee Amendments. When a proposition with committee amendments is returned to the organization bearing the favorable recommendation of the committee, the procedure is as follows: The original proposition is read as a whole and then section by section. Committee amendments are offered at the designated sections. If amendments to committee amendments are offered from the floor, they are allowed. After all committee amendments have been offered, amendments from the floor may be offered and finally the question is on the adoption of the resolution.

76. Treatment of Original Amendments and Committee Amendments. When a proposition referred to a committee with amendments pending is returned to the parent group with committee amendments, the proposition is laid before the organization and the question comes first on the adoption of the amendments pending at the time the main proposition was committed.

Secondary amendments may be offered from the floor to the amendments pending at the time the proposition was referred. After these secondary amendments and the amendments to which they apply have been disposed of, the committee amendments are offered. Secondary amendments which seek to perfect the committee amendments must be allowed. After all committee amendments and secondary amendments offered from the floor have been disposed of, it is in order to offer primary amendments from the floor and then secondary amendments may be offered to these amendments. Finally the question is on the adoption of the resolution as amended.

77. Treatment of Committee Substitute. When a proposition referred to a committee with amendments pending is returned to the organization with a committee substitute for the entire proposition, the procedure is as follows. The question comes first on the adoption of the amendments which were pending at the time of commitment. These amendments may be amended and other amendments to the main proposition may be offered. This procedure allows the proponents of the original proposition to perfect it.* After all amendments seeking to perfect the original proposition have been offered, the presiding officer lays the substitute proposition before the organization. The proponents of the substitute proposition are allowed to perfect it with primary and secondary amendments.** The question then comes on the adoption of the substitute resolution. If the substitute resolution is adopted, the question comes next on the adoption of the resolution as substituted; but if the substitute resolution fails, the question is on the adoption of the original proposition.

78. Matters Originating in Committee. If the resolution or proposition originates in committee, that is when a member or a subcommittee appointed by the

---

*The theory of this is that the original proposition must be perfected before the substitute is offered, since the original proposition cannot be amended after a substitute has been offered and placed before the assembly for consideration.

**All amendments to the substitute must be offered and voted on before the motion to supplant the original by adopting the substitute is voted on.

committee drafts a certain resolution or proposition in accordance with committee instructions, the procedure in committee is as follows:

The entire proposition is read throughout and then read again section by section. When it is being read section by section it is open to amendments. An amendment is voted on but not the paragraph as amended. After each paragraph has been open to amendment and discussion, the entire resolution is open to amendment. Then the proposition is voted on as a whole.

A committee adopts a proposition which it originates but cannot adopt a proposition referred to it. The reason for this difference is that the committee has no authority to adopt or reject a proposition referred to it; it can only recommend. However, the proposition which originates in committee would have no standing in the parent organization unless it was adopted as a whole in the committee. All amendments which were agreed to on a proposition which originated in the committee are incorporated in the proposition and when the proposition is sent to the parent organization, it is as a whole.

When a proposition which originated in committee is sent to the parent group, it is treated as any other main proposition, that is, it is laid before the organization and is open to amendments and all subsidiary motions until it is finally disposed of.

79. **Society's Control of a Committee.** The society may recall a proposition which has been sent to a committee by a motion to reconsider the vote on the motion

to commit and then refusing to commit when the motion to commit is voted on again. Such a motion to reconsider must be made on the same day or on the next day and before the committee to which the proposition was referred has commenced work on it. This motion to reconsider requires a simple majority for adoption.

In the event it is too late to make a motion to reconsider or the committee has commenced work on the proposition referred to it, the parent organization may adopt a motion "that the committee be discharged from further consideration of the proposition." This motion requires a two-thirds vote unless previous notice was given that the motion to discharge would be made. If notice has been given, the motion requires a simple majority for adoption.

COMMITTEE REPORTS

80. **Definition.** A report of a committee is a statement of its findings, or recommendations, or both, upon the matter referred to it.

81. **Accept, Adopt, Agree, Receive.** A committee report is received when it is read and it is never necessary to move that it be received unless the committee wishes to report at some unusual time. A motion to receive the report of the committee when the motion is made in order to allow the committee to report at an unusual time, requires a two-thirds vote, inasmuch as the adoption of the motion suspends the regular order of business. An acceptance of a report is an endorsement or adoption of it, and the motion to accept or the motion to agree should never be made unless the intent

is to adopt the report of the committee as the report of the parent group. A committee report is advisory only. Committees should prepare resolutions to carry out their recommendations. The resolutions must be considered separately and apart from the report itself.* If the report contains findings only it is not necessary for the committee to prepare resolutions, since the report presents information only.

82. **Reception Deferred.** If for any reason the parent group is not ready to receive the report, it may defer the reception since a report is before the assembly for consideration in its regular place in the order of business when it is received.

83. **Reports Withdrawn.** A committee report may be withdrawn before any action is taken, with the permission of the assembly.

84. **Discharging a Committee.** When a special committee has made its final report, the committee ceases to exist. There is no necessity for a motion that the

---

*This text holds that a committee report and the resolutions recommended by the committee in its report should be separate and distinct. The writer is of the opinion that a report should be offered and then the chairman or the member acting for the committee should present the resolution or resolutions one at a time and move their adoption. The reason for this position is that if the report is adopted as a whole, some members may be embarrassed because they might want to vote for some of the resolutions but not all of them. If the report is read only as the advice of the committee and then the resolutions recommended are offered separately, the organization is able to select any or all of the recommendations of the committee without having to accept the report in its entirety.

Robert's Rules of Order, Revised, gives several ways of treating committee reports. It says, Sec. 54, paragraph 3: "If the report concludes with a resolution or a series of resolutions the proper course is for the reporting member to move that the resolution or resolutions be adopted or agreed to. This method should be adopted whenever practicable."

This writer agrees with Robert that this plan is the most practicable.

committee be discharged. When a committee is discharged either automatically or by a motion, all papers pertaining to the deliberations of the committee must be returned to the secretary of the organization.

85. **Form.** Reports of committees take various forms. When the chairman alone signs the report it takes the following form:

Standing committee report:

"May 5, 19—.

"Mr. Chairman:

The committee on ways and means begs leave to recommend the following propositions.

(Propositions attached.)

William Smith, Chairman."

When the members sign the report it takes the following form and the chairman signs as a member without using his title. This is true whether the report be one of a standing or a special committee.

Special committee report:

"May 15, 19—.

"Mr. Chairman:

We, your committee appointed to consider the advisability of changing the system of voting, beg leave to recommend the following propositions.

(Propositions attached.)

Aubrey Jones
Benjamin Smith
Marvin Robinson."

Other Forms:

"May 27, 19—.

"Mr. President:

The committee on housing appointed to investigate places for meeting and to recommend a selection, begs leave to report:

Shriners' Hall ....$50.00 per month
City Auditorium ....$40.00 per month
Odd Fellows' Hall.....................$35.00 per month

Respectfully submitted,

Raymond Lewis, Chairman."

"Mr. President:

The committee on housing offers the following resolution and recommends its adoption:

"Committee Resolution:

Whereas, The Geographic Society is desirous of finding more suitable quarters in which to hold its meetings; and

Whereas, The committee on housing has investigated the available halls, and is of the opinion that the Odd Fellows' Hall would be more suitable to the needs of the organization than any of the others, because of the seating facilities and the low rental; now, therefore, be it

Resolved, That the Geographic Society select the Odd Fellows' Hall as their future meeting place."

"June 2, 19—.

"Mr. President:

The committee on program has studied various programs of work and here reports its findings and recommendation to the assembly:

Program of Work No. 1
    Six lectures on types of soil $200.00
Program of Work No. 2
    Four lectures on the varying
    courses of streams $150.00
Program of Work No. 3
    Study course in the various strata in
    the soil in the Harris Mullen
    Survey $100.00

                Respectfully submitted,
                Eugene Franks, Chairman."

"Mr President:

The committee on program offers the following resolution and recommends its adoption:

Committee Resolution:

Whereas, The committee on program has considered the various programs from the angle of accuracy, application and expense; and

Whereas, The committee finds that the study course in the various strata of the soil in the Harris Mullen Survey meets the requirements of the Geographic Society as to accuracy, personal application, and expense; now, therefore, be it

Resolved, That the Geographic Society adopt the pro-

gram of work relating to the strata of soil in the Harris
Mullen Survey."

"July 30, 19——.

"Mr. President:

Your committee on resolutions begs leave to report
the following resolutions with the recommendation that
they do pass:

Resolution No. 1, relating to the convention,

Resolution No. 2, relating to the drive for members,

Resolution No. 3, relating to official cars during the
convention,

Resolution No. 4, relating to entertainment for visiting
delegates.

Respectfully submitted,
Alathea Lewis, Chairman."

86. **Reception of Report.** If a proposition or resolution has been referred to a committee by the parent
body and the committee returns it with a report, the
report is read. The report may take many forms. It
may recommend that the proposition do pass with
committee amendments, or simply that it do pass or
that it do not pass. Regardless of the kind of report
the committee makes, the question is on the adoption
of the proposition. If committee amendments are
offered, the question comes first on the adoption of
the committee amendments and then on the adoption
of the proposition if no further amendments are offered. The committee report is advisory only and if
it recommends that the proposition do not pass, the committee has served its purpose when it advised the society.

The question is always the affirmative one, that is, "on the adoption of the proposition referred."

87. Minority Report. When a minority of a committee differs from the committee it can express its views in either of two forms. The report of the minority on a committee cannot be offered until the proposition to which it applies and the committee report are laid before the assembly. It is then in order for a member of the minority to seek to have the views of the minority read. If there is objection, a motion may be made to receive or hear the minority view. Such a motion is not debatable.

(1)   The report may be in this form:

"We, the undersigned, a minority of the committee selected to recommend a plan for financing the erection of a clubhouse, not agreeing with the majority, wish to recommend the following plan for financing the project.

Frank Smith
Aubrey Harris

Resolution attached."

If the assembly permits the views of the minority to be read it is in order to move to substitute their resolution for the resolution recommended by the committee report.* The procedure is the same as that outlined in Section 77, p. 124. If, however, the assembly should

---

*This text differs from Robert's Rules of Order, Revised, in that Robert allows the minority report to be substituted for the report of the committee. This author allows the resolution or proposition proposed by the minority to be offered as a substitute for the resolution or proposition as offered by the committee because the procedure is simpler and much more direct.

not permit the views of the minority to be read, the minority resolution could be offered as a substitute by any member.

(2)   The views of the minority may be expressed in this form:

"Mr. Chairman:

"We, the undersigned, a minority of your committee on ways and means, recommend that the resolution Number 10, referred to the committee on ways and means, do not pass.

Frank Smith
Aubrey Harris."

88. **Reception of Minority Report.** When the report of the ways and means committee is laid before the assembly with the recommendation that a resolution do pass and a so-called minority report recommending that the resolution do not pass is offered, the question is on the adoption of the resolution, not on the adoption of the minority report or the substitution of the minority report for the majority report, inasmuch as committee reports are advisory only.

Both the committee report and the minority report are entered upon the minutes of the journal and become a part of the proceedings.

STUDY AND DISCUSSION TOPICS

1.   Why are committees important?

2.   Name the five classes of committees and tell which classes you would expect to find in the following organizations?
Commercial stock company,
Religious institution,
Legislative body,
Study club,
Mass meeting,
Political convention.

3.   Compare procedure in committee of the whole, quasi-committee of the whole, and in the organization proper.

4.   When a committee report is presented to the assembly, is a motion that it be received necessary?

5.   Describe the procedure of presenting and acting on committee reports.

6.   What is the effect of adjournment *sine die* on committees and on unfinished business?

7.   Is a committee permitted to adopt a resolution referred to it? An amendment referred to it? A resolution it originates? An amendment it originates?

8.   How is a committee substitute acted on in committee and in the assembly?

9.   Give examples of the several forms of committee reports.

10. Discuss the treatment of the views of the minority of a committee.

CHAPTER VI.

ORGANIZATION ROUTINE

SESSION

89. **Definition.** A session of an organization is a meeting or a group of adjourned or recessed meetings which are regarded as one continuous conference or convention. The session may or may not adjourn *sine die.**

Many organizations define the duration of a session in their organic law.

A convention is in reality one session although it may recess or adjourn from day to day. Such meetings are termed adjourned meetings and do not constitute a session in themselves, being a continuation

---

*A *sine die* adjournment is one which closes a particular session for which no other meeting has been provided.

Conventions, when they have completed their work, adjourn *sine die* since that particular convention will not meet again. Legislative bodies adjourn *sine die* if they do not have regular session dates, as they cannot meet again unless called by the President or the Governor.

The motion to adjourn *sine die* is not made in organizations for which regular meetings are provided. When a motion to adjourn *sine die* is adopted in a temporary or mass meeting, the meeting can never be called together again.

of the meeting that provided the adjourned meeting. An adjournment to meet another day ends that particular meeting but does not affect the continuity of the meetings that make the session. Any meeting that is not an adjourned meeting of some other meeting constitutes a new session.

Examples: (a) The several state legislatures and the Congress of the United States often stay in session several months at a time. The recesses and adjournments from day to day neither end the session nor affect the progress of business, as the recessed meetings and the adjourned meetings are a part of the whole session.

(b) In an organization that has meetings at definite meeting periods, each meeting is a session unless the rules of the organization provide otherwise.

90. **Limitation on Sessions.** It is not wise for a session to include too many meetings as it would prevent many motions and propositions from being considered again until that session was over and a new one started.

Examples: (a) If a main motion is laid on the table during one session, the same motion or an identical one cannot be considered again at that particular session unless the motion is taken from the table. If a proposition is postponed indefinitely or rejected at one session, the same or a similar proposition cannot be considered during the same session. Both propositions can be introduced and considered anew at a later session.

(b) A motion to reconsider which was made at the last meeting of a session but never disposed of, can be called up for action at the next session. However, it is not in order to move to reconsider a vote taken during the prior session. If on the last meeting day of a session a motion to reconsider is made but not disposed of, the assembly may follow one of two courses of action: (1) dispose of the motion to reconsider in a later session; (2) provide for an adjourned meeting and dispose of the motion to reconsider. If the proposition is one on which action should not be suspended, the motion to reconsider should be disposed of when made or an adjourned meeting provided for the purpose of disposing of the motion.

RENEWAL OF A MOTION

91. **Motions that Can Be Renewed.** The ordinary rule is that when any main motion has been adopted or rejected at one particular session, it cannot be offered again at the same session.

The following motions cannot be renewed at the same session which refused them unless they were made and withdrawn before any action was taken on them: (1) to adopt a main motion, (2) to postpone indefinitely a main motion, (3) to adopt an amendment, (4) to reconsider the second time unless the motion was amended when previously reconsidered, (5) to object to the consideration of the question, (6) to fix the time to which to adjourn, (7) to suspend the rules for the same purpose at the same meeting.*

The motions to adjourn, to take a recess, to take from the table, the call for the orders of the day, and

---

*A motion to suspend the rules on some particular proposition may not be renewed at the same meeting though it can be renewed on the same day but in a different meeting.

all of the subsidiary motions, except the motions to postpone indefinitely and to amend, can be renewed after progress in debate. Legislative bodies have held that debate is progress. Many organizations hold that some progress other than debate must have been made before these motions can be renewed.

EFFECT OF ADJOURNMENT

92. **Effect of Adjournment on Organic Law.** The rules of order, the by-laws, and the constitution are binding from one session to another or until they have been amended. Previous notice of the amendments to be considered must have been given before they can be considered. Standing rules of one session can be suspended in another session by majority vote.

93. **Effect of Adjournment on Committees.** The end of the meeting or session has no effect on committees which have been appointed to report at a future time.

94. **Effect of Adjournment on Unfinished Business.** The effect of adjournment on unfinished business depends upon the type of session or meeting to which the motion applies. If the motion to adjourn does not end the session and is simply a motion to adjourn to another meeting, it only interrupts the discussion on the matter or proposition. The pending business at adjournment is taken up at the time for unfinished business at the next meeting and unfinished business always comes before new business.

If the motion to adjourn applies to a monthly or weekly meeting of an organization, the pending business goes over as unfinished business to the next regular meeting of the organization and is taken up before the new business unless the next meeting begins a new session. If the next meeting begins a new session, all unfinished business of the old session dies and must be introduced again at the new session.

One committee or board of directors cannot pass unfinished business on to a new committee or new board of directors if the entire committee or board of directors is new.

MEETING

95. **Definition.** A meeting is a group of people engaged in deliberation for a length of time without an adjournment. A meeting may be a session as well as a meeting, or it may be one meeting that is a part of a session. Any meeting which commences anew (that is, one that is not an adjournment of another meeting or a recessed meeting) begins a new session. (Section 89, p. 135.)

96. **Types of Meetings.** There are three types of meetings: (1) Regular (2) Special (3) Annual.

The constitution should provide the dates of the regular meetings, the manner in which a special meeting can be called, and the date of the annual meeting. The by-laws should provide the hour of the regular meetings.

97. **Considered in a Regular Meeting.** A regular meeting of an organization can transact any business not in conflict with its constitution, its by-laws, rules of order, standing rules, or the laws of the country.

98. **Considered in a Special Meeting.** A special meeting can consider only that matter for which the meeting was

called. The minutes of a regular meeting should not be read at a special meeting unless the reading and approval of the minutes was included in the call.

99. Order of Business in a Special Meeting.

(1) Call to order
(2) Reading of the call
(3) Consideration of the matter
     named in the call
(4) Adjournment

100. Considered in an Annual Meeting. An annual meeting is a summary of the year's work in that all officers and chairmen of committees make their reports for the year. Officers and members of the board of directors for the coming year are elected at this meeting if the constitution so provides.

101. Order of Business in an Annual Meeting.

(1) Call to order
(2) Annual report of officers
(3) Annual report of committee chairmen
(4) Reports of special committees
(5) Nominations and election of officers
(6) Miscellaneous business
(7) Reading and approval of the minutes
     of the present session
(8) Adjournment

102. Adjourned Meeting. If the business of any meeting is not completed in one meeting, the assembly may provide for an adjourned meeting by moving that the organization adjourn until a certain time or by adopting a motion to fix the time to which to adjourn and later adjourning. Such a meeting is always a continuation of the meeting which provided for the adjourned one. Any business that would have been in order at the first meeting is in order at the adjourned meeting.

103. **Providing Time for Adjourned Meetings.** If it is necessary to provide for an adjourned meeting to consider some matter, the time for the adjourned meeting should be set before the matter is postponed to that day.

QUORUM

104. **Definition.** A quorum is the number of members whose presence is necessary to transact business legally. It is always a majority of the members of an organization or of an assembly unless the rules provide otherwise. Frequently in large organizations a number less than a majority makes a quorum because it is difficult to get a majority of the members of a large society together at one time.

105. **How Provided for.** A quorum should be provided for in the constitution of the organization. When a quorum is less than a majority, rules should specify the time and place of meeting so that the organization cannot divide into two assemblies. Members present but not voting are counted to make a quorum.

106. **Action in Absence of a Quorum.** The chair should wait until a quorum is present before he calls the meeting to order unless there is evidence that there will not be a quorum. In such event, the chair should call

the meeting to order and entertain a motion to adjourn or a motion for a call of the house when the organization permits this procedure.

107. Raising the Point of "No Quorum." A quorum is presumed to be present until the question is raised, and the question cannot be raised while a member is speaking. The question of "no quorum" is a matter of general privilege. The member noticing the lack of a quorum rises and addresses the chair:

Member: "Mr. Chairman, I rise to a question of general privilege."

The Chair: "State your question of privilege."

Member: "I make the point of 'no quorum.'"

108. Determining the Lack of a Quorum. After the point of "no quorum" is made, the chair must find out whether or not a quorum is present by appointing tellers to count the members or by ordering a roll call.

109. Effect of Lack of Quorum. When it is found that a quorum is not present no motion is in order* except to adjourn, to fix the time to which to adjourn, or to order a call of the house.** Debate may continue on a proposition, but no vote on it is in order. Unanimous

---

*This text differs from Robert's Rules of Order Revised in that Robert allows an assembly to recess when the lack of a quorum has been determined. This text does not allow a recess to be taken after a lack of quorum has been determined because there is no count or roll call at the beginning of a recessed meeting, and consequently no occasion for determining the presence of a quorum. After the lack of a quorum has been determined, no vote is legal until the record, journal or minutes shows that a count has been taken and that there is a quorum present.

**The organization must have a special rule to permit call of the house.

consent when there is no quorum present has no effect or standing.

110. Quorum in Committee of the Whole. A quorum in the committee of the whole is the same as a quorum in the organization proper. The procedure in committees when there is no quorum is the same as in organizations: nothing can be done except to rise, although debate may continue on a proposition after the point of "no quorum" is made but no vote can be taken.

No committee, board, or other group can take action without a quorum.

ORDER OF BUSINESS

111. Definition. Order of business usually means a certain schedule which an assembly has adopted either in a permanent society or in a temporary meeting. The order of business may be written in the by-laws or in the rules of order. (Section 26, Art. 5, p. 99.)

112. General and Special Orders. A special order is considered at the hour appointed for its consideration; a general order cannot interfere with the regular rules of the assembly and must wait its turn in the order of business.

It is not in order to take up any general or special order before the time to which it was appointed except by a two-thirds vote. A general order or even a special order can be postponed by a majority vote when it comes up for consideration. The general order so postponed loses nothing of its preference, but a special order postponed by a majority vote becomes a general order.

If two special orders were made for the same hour, the one made first is considered first. General orders made for the same day are considered in the order in which they were made.

113. Introduction of Business. Business is brought before the assembly by the making of a motion, the reading of a paper, a matter of privilege, or a petition.

The person who wishes to bring any matter before the assembly must first obtain recognition from the presiding officer.* This is done by the person's addressing the chair in this manner:

Member: "Mr. Chairman, Mr. Brown of the Sumner District speaking."

The Chair: (If he recognizes the person.) "Mr. Brown," or perhaps, "The delegate from the Sumner District."

After the person has been recognized by the presiding officer, he proceeds with the motion, paper, or matter of privilege that he wishes the assembly to consider.

The presiding officer may at any time require that all matters submitted for consideration be in writing.

114. Petition. The right of petition originated in the United States with a guarantee of the right of petition by the Constitution. A petition is a prayer for a grant or for some specific action addressed to the body that has

---

*The motions or questions which can be made without obtaining recognition are:

  (1) Objection to the consideration of the question
  (2) Call for orders of the day
  (3) Call to order
  (4) Questions of privilege
  (5) Appeals
  (6) Amend by filling blanks

jurisdiction over the matters included in the petition. It is usually signed by numerous persons. When it is presented the substance of the petition should be stated.

Resolutions may be offered complying with the request in the petition.

NOMINATIONS

115. When Made. Nominations are made when nominations are declared to be open. The chair may declare nominations to be open or a member may move to open nominations.

116. Determining the Method of Making Nominations. Usually the organic law designates which method shall be employed in making nominations. If no rule of the organization states the method, any member may make a motion prescribing the method to be used. When an election is pending, the motion to fix the method of making nominations is an incidental motion and undebatable. When no election is pending, the motion is an incidental main motion and is debatable. (See Sections 172 and 238, pp. 178 and 256-7.)

117. Methods of Making Nominations. Nominations may be made in the following ways:

(1) From the floor
(2) By a nominating committee
(3) By ballot
(4) By mail
(5) By the chair*

---

*If nominations are to be made by the chair, the assembly must authorize such procedure. The chair may nominate several persons for the office and the assembly then elects from this list of nominees.

118. Nominations from the Floor. Nominations made from the floor are not amendments; so they are not limited in number as are amendments. They do not require a second.* Any members may make a nomination, but no member may make more than one nomination for the same office without general consent. The presiding officer repeats the nominations in the order of their making and the secretary keeps a record of the order in which the nominations are made. When the nominations are closed, the chair puts each nomination to the vote until one of the nominees receives a majority vote, unless the rules of the organization provide for more than a majority vote to elect, in which case the balloting continues until a nominee has received the sufficient number of votes.

119. Closing Nominations. Nominations are closed when no one wishes to make another nomination or when a motion is made that nominations be closed and is adopted by a two-thirds vote. It is not in order for the chair to close nominations until every one who wishes has had an opportunity to make a nomination. A motion to reopen nominations may be made and is adopted by a majority vote.

When nominations are made to fill several places of equal rank, as members of a committee, and the number of persons nominated is exactly the number required, all shall be voted on at one time. If more nominations are made than the vacancies require, the voting shall be done individually.

---

*See footnote on page 32.

120. Nomination by Committee. If the constitution or by-laws provide for nominations to be made by the nominating committee, or if a motion is adopted choosing this method of nomination, the nominating committee reports with one or more names for each office, according to the instructions given them. Nominations made by committee have the same standing as those made from the floor if the constitution so provides. Further nominations from the floor may be made after the committee has reported unless the constitution or by-laws have provided another manner of making additional nominations.

121. Nomination by Ballot. When the authority for nominations provides that nominations shall be by ballot, the members of the organization nominate their preferences for office by ballot. When nominations are made by ballot, no nominations from the floor are permitted.

In small organizations it may be possible to vote on all the nominations made by ballot; in large organizations a rule should be made to determine the number of nominees and the way they are to be selected.

122. Nomination by Mail. This form of nominating is most often used by groups located at a distance from a parent organization. Each group may nominate by mail. If this method of nominating is used, provision for it must be made in the constitution or by-laws.

STUDY AND DISCUSSION TOPICS

1.   Why is it well to have a limit on the length of a session?

2.   What is an adjourned meeting? How is it provided?

3.   What is a quorum? How does the presiding officer know what percentage of membership constitutes a quorum in the organization?

4.   What is the effect of finding that a quorum is not present?

5.   Define the term "meeting". Name the three types of meetings.

6.   How are nominations made from the floor.

7.   Name five ways of making nominations. What method do you recommend for nomination of permanent officers? Why?

8.   Define the expression, "order of business".

9.   How and when is business brought before an assembly?

10.   What purpose does a petition serve?

CHAPTER VII.

DEBATE

DEFINITION OF DEBATE

123. **Definition.** Debate is the discussion of any subject which is introduced to the assembly. The subject is introduced by means of a motion or a proposition which must be a debatable one if debate is to follow.

No proposition is open for debate until it has been seconded* and stated by the presiding officer.

---

*The following motions do not require a second:

(1) Objection to the consideration of a question
(2) Call to order
(3) Call for the orders of the day
(4) Nominations
(5) Leave to withdraw a motion
(6) Inquiries of any kind
(7) Amend by filling blanks
(8) Questions of order
(9) Questions of privilege
(10) Call up a motion to reconsider
(11) Call for a division of the question (under certain conditions).

PRINCIPLES OF RECOGNITION

124. **Obtaining the Floor.** The person who wishes to bring any matter before the assembly must first obtain recognition from the presiding officer.*

125. **Length of Speeches in Debate.** No person may speak more than once on any proposition nor longer than ten minutes without the permission of the assembly, except that the maker of a motion or the person acting for a committee may open the debate with a twenty-minute speech and may close it with a twenty-minute speech. No member shall be permitted to use the time of another member without the consent of the assembly.

126. **Appeal from the Decision of the Chair as to Recognition.** In legislative assemblies, no appeal from the chair as to recognition is permitted. However, in voluntary bodies, an appeal from the decision of the chair as to who is entitled to prior recognition is permitted.

127. **Rights When One Has the Floor.** After a person has obtained recognition and has the floor, he cannot be interrupted except by:

(1) A motion to reconsider and spread on the minutes
(2) A question of order
(3) An objection to the consideration of the question
(4) A call for the orders of the day

---

*See footnote to section 113, page 144 for motions which may be made without obtaining recognition.

(5) A question of urgent privilege

(6) A request to yield made by
another member

(7) A motion to reconsider.

The speaker may refuse to yield to the question of another member, but the making of the motions and exceptions listed here are matters of higher rank and can interrupt a speaker without his consent.

128. **Priority of Recognition.** When two or more persons who are seeking recognition rise and address the chair, the presiding officer must determine which one he will recognize. These principles of recognition are most often used:

(1) If the maker of the motion or the person who brought the pending matter before the assembly has not spoken on the proposition, the chair should recognize him in preference to others who may be seeking the floor. This is true even though in reality another person addressed the chair before the maker of the motion.

(2) The chair should not recognize persons who have already spoken on a proposition if there is another person seeking recognition who has not spoken on the proposition.

(3) If the presiding officer knows the speakers and their opinions of a measure, he may well alternate the recognition between those favoring a proposition and those opposed to it. It is permissible for the chair to ask of a person who is seeking recognition whether he wishes to speak for or against the matter before he recognizes him. This should be followed provided the

person who is seeking recognition does not fall within the two exceptions mentioned above.

The mover of a proposition or the person reporting a matter for a committee has the right to speak on the matter first if he so desires. He has the right also to speak last after every member who wishes to speak has spoken unless he has exhausted his time or unless debate is cut off by the motion for the previous question or by a motion to limit or close debate. He can vote against his measure, but he is not permitted to speak against it.

DECORUM

129. **Decorum in Debate.** When the presiding officer stands to give information or to make a decision, the member who has the floor should take his seat. During debate, the officers of the organization or assembly should always be referred to by their official titles. It is not in order to call names during debate. If a person wishes to refer to some person he may describe the person.

130. **Objection to Speaker's Remarks.** Personalities should be avoided in debate. The measures rather than the members who introduce them should be debated. If a member objects to the remarks of a speaker, he should take them down and either call the person to order during his speech or present the matter immediately after the speaker has finished. The organization is the judge of the propriety of the speaker's remarks and may ask him to apologize to the member offended.

Should he refuse to do so the organization may deal with him. If the words objected to are of a personal nature, both parties to the offense should retire before the assembly considers the matter.

131. Permission to Continue Remarks. If the member objecting interrupts a speaker with a matter of privilege and the organization holds that the speaker's remarks have been improper, he may not continue his remarks without the permission of the assembly.

132. Objection Must Be Made Immediately. If any business has been transacted since the disorderly words were used, it is not in order for the person objecting to present the matter to the assembly.

133. Debate Must Be Pertinent. A speaker must confine his remarks to the question then pending; that is, if he is speaking on an amendment, he must confine his remarks to the amendment unless it is of such nature that its adoption would destroy the purpose or effectiveness of the main motion. All remarks should be addressed to the chair.

134. Personal Interest. When any matter comes before the assembly in which a member has a personal interest, he should make his interest known to the assembly and refuse to vote on the matter.

135. Withdrawal of a Second or a Motion. When a motion is altered by the maker before it is stated by the chair, the person who seconded the original motion may withdraw his second if he wishes to do so. The maker of a motion may alter his motion or even withdraw it before it is stated by the chair; but once it is stated by the chair, he cannot withdraw it, if anyone objects, without the permission of the assembly. (Section 232, p. 250.)

136. Duties of the Chair Concerning Debate. The chair may aid the maker of the motion by asking questions about the purpose of the motion and advising him of the proper form. Sometimes it is helpful to allow a little informal talk concerning the form and purpose of the motion before it is stated for discussion, even on undebatable questions. This does not mean that debate should be permitted before the motion is stated. If the chair asks advice on a question of order, the member should give the advice while seated, to avoid the appearance of a debate. One who merely asks a question or makes a suggestion does not lose his right to debate.

The presiding officer should always allow opportunity for debate and should in no way permit his feelings on a matter to influence his actions as a presiding officer. (For conditions under which the presiding officer may join in debate, see section 33, p. 102.)

The chair cannot close debate as long as any member wishes to speak. If a member rises to seek recognition and the chair, failing to see him, puts the question to a vote, the member shall be recognized after the vote has been taken, and may speak on the proposition as though the vote had never been taken. The chair again puts the question to a vote. Or if the affirmative vote has been taken, a member seeking recognition must be recognized for debate before the question is completed. If the chair gave enough opportunity for debate after asking, "Are you ready for the question?" members cannot claim the privilege of debate after the voting has commenced. These rules do not hold when debate has been cut off by the adoption of one of the motions that limit or cut off debate. When a vote is being taken by roll call and the roll call has commenced, debate may not be renewed, nor may debate be renewed during division of the house.

MOTIONS AFFECTING DEBATE

137. Motions in Order during Debate. Immediately after introduction of a proposition or after partial debate the following motions may be made:

(1) Make a special order. (Section 241, p. 259 and Section 195, p. 212.)

(2) Lay on the table. (Section 186, p. 200.)

(3) Previous question. (Section 187, p. 203.)

(4) Limit or close debate. (Section 234, p.252.)

(5) Postpone to a certain time. (Section 194, p. 209.)

(6) Commit, refer, or recommit. (Section 196, p. 214.)

(7) Refer to committee of the whole, quasi-committee of the whole, or consider informally. (Sections 48-61, pp. 110-115.)

(8) Permit reading of papers. (Section 231, p. 249.)

(9) Amend, any form. (Section 202, p. 218.)

(10) Fix method of voting when a proposition is pending. (Section 237, p. 256.)

(11) Postpone indefinitely. (Section 216, p. 230.)

138. Tactics That Must Be Used Immediately. Some motions and objections must be made *immediately*, as soon as the occasion arises. The occasion may be the introduction of a motion, a question of order, a question of privilege, a matter of appointment or election, or a matter of personal consideration. Motions and objections that must be made immediately are:

(1) Calling a member or speaker to order. (Section 228, p. 244.)

(2) Rising to a question of privilege upon the infringements of rights. (Sections 221-224, pp. 237-241.)

(3) Objection to a member's speaking again to a question before others have spoken. (Section 128, part 2, p. 151.)

(4) Objection to a member's continuing in speech or conduct after indecorum in debate. (Section 132, p. 153.)

(5) Objection to offensive words or conduct. (Sections 130 & 228, pp. 152 & 244.)

(6) Questioning the right to proceed because a motion was not seconded. (Section 228, p. 244.)

(7) Questioning the action of the chair in changing the wording of a motion when stating or putting it. (Section 228, p. 244.)

(8) A motion or question concerning the priority of business. (Sections 225 & 228 pp. 241 & 244.)

(9) Objection to the consideration of a question. (Section 230, p. 248.)

(10) Objection to the reception of a report. (Section 82, p. 127.)

(11) Declining a nomination. (Section 43, p. 107.)

(12) Declining to serve in office or on a committee. (Section 43, p. 107.)

(13) Declining to perform any duty assigned. (Section 43, p. 107.)

(14) An appeal from the decision of the chair. (Section 229, p. 246.)

139. **Motions That Open the Merits of the Main Question to Debate.**

(1) To postpone indefinitely. (Section 216, p. 230.)

(2) To rescind. (Section 177, p. 182.)

(3) To reconsider a debatable question. (Section 179, p. 184.)

(4) To ratify. (Section 185, p. 196.)

140. **Motions That Limit or Cut Off Debate:**

(1) Previous question (Section 187, p. 203.)

(2) Objection to consideration (Section 230, p. 248.)

(3) Close or limit debate (Section 234, p. 252.)

(4) Lay on the table (Section 186, p. 200.)

141. **Motions That Suppress a Question.**

(1) Objection to the consideration of the question. (Section 230, p. 248.)

(2) Postpone indefinitely. (Section 216, p. 230.)

(3) Lay on the table. (Section 186, p. 200.)

142. **Questions That Are Undebatable.**

(1) Fix the time to which the assembly shall adjourn, when privileged. (Section 218, p. 233.)

(2) Adjourn, when privileged, (Section 219, p. 234.)

or to rise in committee of the whole. (Section 52,p. 112.)

(3) Take a recess, when privileged. (Section 220, p. 236.)

(4) Call for the orders of the day and all questions relating to the priority of business. (Sections 225 & 228, pp. 241 & 244.)

(5) An undebatable appeal. (Section 229, p. 246.)

(6) Objection to the consideration of a question. (Section 230, p. 248.)

(7) A motion to lay on the table (Section 186, p. 200.) or take from the table. (Section 181, p. 192.)

(8) The motion for the previous question. (Section 187, p. 203.)

(9) The motion to divide the question. (Section 242, p. 260.)

(10) The motion to reconsider an undebatable question. (Section 179, p. 184.)

(11) A motion to amend an undebatable question. (Section 202, p. 218.)

(12) A motion to grant permission to read papers. (Section 231, p. 249.)

(13) A motion to suspend the rules. (Section 233, p. 251.)

(14) A motion to withdraw a motion. (Section 232, p. 250.)

(15) A motion to limit or close debate. (Section 234, p. 252.)

(16) A motion to extend the limits of debate. (Section 235, p. 254.)

(17) A motion to give one permission to continue his

remarks after he has been found guilty of indecorum in debate. (Section 239, p. 257.)

(18) All incidental motions except appeal, questions of order, and approve or correct the minutes. (Section 167, p. 172; Section 228, p. 244; and Section 236, p. 255.)

STUDY AND DISCUSSION TOPICS

1. What must be done before debate on a proposition can begin?

2. When several members rise to be recognized for debate at the same time, how shall the chair determine which to recognize first.

3. If a member thinks that the chair has been unfair in refusing him recognition, what can he do?

4. May a member interrupt a speaker?

5. If a speaker makes objectionable personal remarks, how is he dealt with?

6. When is it proper for a member to remain seated while addressing the chair?

7. What motions and objections must be made immediately?

8. Give an example of introducing a motion, dramatizing the procedure, closing with the chair putting the question to a vote.

9. What motions and questions can interrupt a member who has the floor?

10. Classify motions as to purpose.

CHAPTER VIII.

VOTING

FORMS OF VOTING

143. **Definition.** Voting is the manner by which the prevailing opinion of a group is determined.

144. **Forms.** Voting takes many forms according to the type of motion, proposition, or election before the assembly. The ordinary methods of voting are:

(1) Acclamation, general consent, silent consent, and unanimous consent. (Sections 145-146, pp. 160-161.)

(2) *Viva voce* vote. (Section 147, p. 161.)

(3) Raising the hand. (Section 148, p. 162.)

(4) Division of the house. (Section 149, p. 162.)

(5) Ballot. (Section 151, p. 163.)

(6) Roll call. (Section 152, p. 163.)

145. **Voting by Acclamation.** Acclamation is a vocal vote. It is used only when there is one candidate for an office. If there is a rule in the organization that election be by ballot, it is not in order to move that election be by acclamation or that the secretary cast the unanimous vote of the assembly.

A motion that the candidate be elected by acclamation

if adopted merely fixes the method of voting. Another vote is required to elect.

In voting to extend thanks or to acknowledge favors, if there is a fair showing of an affirmative vote, the negative vote is not called for and the vote is assumed to be by acclamation as a mark of courtesy.

146. General Consent, Silent Consent, and Unanimous Consent are used interchangeably to mean a silent affirmative vote, or simply a lack of objection.

Unanimous consent may be asked by any member. The form is:

Member: "Mr. Chairman, I ask unanimous consent to have this memorial read to the assembly."

The Chair: "The member asks unanimous consent to have the memorial read. Is there any objection?"

If there is objection, unanimous consent fails.

The chair very often makes use of general consent in this manner:

"If there is no objection, the chair will defer laying this matter before the assembly until an opinion is had from the parliamentarian."

If there is objection, general consent fails and the chair must lay the matter before the organization.

Parliamentary rules relating to the transaction of routine business and to ordinary matters may be dispensed with by general consent without a vote.

147. Voting by Viva Voce Vote. This is the oral vote: "As many as favor the adoption of the resolution will say 'aye.' "

When the ayes are taken, the question is completed by saying, "As many as are opposed to the adoption of the resolution will say 'no.'"

If no other method of voting is provided by the organic law or by a motion made to fix the method, the chair usually puts the question to a *viva voce* vote. After this vote if the chair or any member feels doubt as to the result of the *viva voce* vote, a vote to determine the accuracy of the result of the voting may be demanded. This second vote is usually taken by raising the hand or some other form of division of the house.

148. **Voting by Raising the Hand.** This is the raising of the hand to determine the number of ayes and noes. It is in reality a form of division.

149. **Voting by Division of the House.** If the chair doubts the result of a *viva voce* vote or a vote by raising of hands, or if a division is called for, the chair should so state and ask those favoring the resolution to rise and stand until the tellers have counted them. When the tellers report the number standing, he should announce the number of ayes and then ask the noes to stand until counted. Then he announces the number of noes and whether the proposition was adopted or failed of adoption.

The chair may count the votes, ask the secretary to count them, or appoint tellers. If he appoints tellers, he should select them from both the affirmative and the negative sides. Tellers appointed to count votes should not count their own votes, but should report to the chair on which side they wish to be counted.

150. **Any Member May Call for a Division of the House.** If a vote was taken *viva voce*, it is permissible to call for a division at any time even after the vote has been announced and another has the floor, but the division must be called for before another motion is made. If a member, absent at the time the vote was taken, returns to the room it is too late to call for a division.

151. **Voting by Ballot.** When the assembly wishes to vote by ballot, a motion to that effect is in order unless the rules of the organization provide otherwise. Voting by ballot is prescribed for elections in many societies where secrecy is desired.

Slips of paper or blanks are distributed among the members who write "aye" or "no" on the blanks, or the name of the person preferred in the case of a nomination or an election. If the vote is on nominees for office, the members are not restricted to the persons nominated but may write in whomsoever they please.

The tellers collect the ballots, count them, and report the result to the chairman. The chair then announces the vote to the assembly in this manner: "A total number of 147 votes were cast. Mr. A. received 127 votes; Mr. B. received 12 votes; Mr. C. received 8 votes. Mr. A., having received a majority of all votes cast, is elected president."

When the vote is by ballot, no member may change his vote.

152. **Voting by Roll Call.** Voting by roll call is the method used when a majority of the members demand

a roll call on the matter.* If a motion to vote by roll call is adopted, the chairman directs the clerk or the secretary to call the roll. On such a vote the chair states the question in this manner:

The Chair: "The question is on the adoption of the resolution to change the name of the ways and means committee to the committee on finance. As many as favor the adoption of the resolution will vote 'aye'; those opposed to the adoption will vote 'no.' The clerk will call the roll."

After the roll call the clerk reports the result to the presiding officer who then announces it to the assembly.

After a roll call has commenced it is too late to ask to be excused from voting.

153. Determining the Form of Voting to Be Used. When there is no rule to determine the method of voting and a question is pending, the incidental motion to fix the method of voting is in order. It can be amended. It is not debatable and requires a majority vote (Section 237, p. 256). If no question is pending, the motion to fix the method of voting is an incidental main motion (Section 173, p. 179).

GENERAL RULES

154. Change of Vote. Change of vote is allowed up to the time the vote is finally announced unless the vote is by ballot. Even after the vote is announced, change of the vote may be permitted by general consent. If there

---

*In legislative assemblies voting by roll call may be called for by a very small number.

is objection, a motion may be made to grant the permission; this motion is undebatable.

155. Personal Interest. A member having a personal interest in a proposition should let it be known and should ask to be excused from voting on it. A member is permitted to vote for himself for office but from delicacy he should not do so except when his vote would change the result. When other members are included with him in the motion he may vote even though his interest is personal.

156. Proxy Voting. A proxy is a power of attorney given by a member to another authorizing him to vote in the member's place. This is rarely used in any but stock companies and business corporations. Because extensive use of it makes debate and deliberation useless, proxy voting is not permissible unless provision for it is made in the organic law.

157. Putting the Question. When an undebatable motion is made, the chairman states the question and puts it to a vote immediately. When the motion is debatable, the chair always asks if the assembly is ready for the question before he puts it to a vote.

VOTES REQUIRED FOR ADOPTION

158. Specifications for Votes. There are four specifications for the number of votes required to adopt a motion or proposition. They are:

(1) Majority.

(2) Two-thirds of the votes cast, ignoring blanks.

(3) Two-thirds of the members present.

(4) Two-thirds vote of the entire membership.

A majority vote is necessary for all motions except those that in effect suspend the regular order of business or those for which the organic law specifies another number of votes. By majority is meant any number more than half of the votes cast, ignoring blanks, when a quorum is present.

In rare instances persons elected to office are elected by a plurality vote. A plurality vote is the highest number of votes where more than two candidates offer for election and no one receives a majority of all votes cast.

Several motions require a two-thirds vote for adoption. This means two-thirds of the votes cast, ignoring blanks, unless otherwise specified. Whenever either two-thirds of the entire membership or two-thirds of the members present is intended, it should be so stated. A two-thirds vote of the entire membership is rarely used except in legislative bodies where the constitution requires that some motions be adopted by two-thirds vote of the entire membership.

159. Motions That Require a Two-Thirds Vote.

(1) Amend the constitution. (Section 180, p. 191.)

(2) Amend the by-laws. (Section 180, p. 191.)

(3) Amend the rules of order. (Section 180, p. 191.)

(4) Suspend the rules. (Section 233, p. 251.)

(5) Close or limit debate. (Section 234, p. 252.)

(6) Extend limits of debate. (Section 235, p. 254.)

(7) Previous question. (Section 187, p. 203.)

(8) Make a special order. (Section 184, p. 195 & Section 195, p. 212 & Section 241, p. 259.)

(9) Take up any subject out of its regular order. (Section 112, p. 143.)

(10) Objection to the consideration of a question. (Section 230, p. 248.)

(11) Expel a member. (Section 160, p. 167.)

160. Expulsion of Members. No member should be expelled by less than a two-thirds vote, a quorum voting. If the member has had charges preferred against him by a committee, the committee members are permitted to vote. Unless general consent is obtained to fix some other method, the vote on expulsion should be by ballot.

161. Elections. Elections are held by the rules laid down in the organic law for the conduct of elections. If no provision has been made, the organization may adopt a motion which provides the method.

STUDY AND DISCUSSION TOPICS

1. May a member vote against a motion he has made? Under what circumstances might he wish to do so?

2. Should a nominee for an office act as teller in an election?

3. May a motion for a different method of voting be made after voting has begun?

4. Name the several methods of voting. Illustrate each method.

5. Who determines the method of voting?

6. What is proxy voting? In what type of organization is it most often used?

7. What is meant by the following terms:
   majority,
   two-thirds of the votes cast ignoring blanks,
   two-thirds of the members present,
   two-thirds of the entire membership?

8. What is the nature of the resolutions and motions that require a two-thirds vote for adoption?

9. What general principle in parliamentary law necessitates that these motions and resolutions require a two-thirds vote?

CHAPTER IX.

GENERAL CLASSIFICATION OF MOTIONS

DEFINITION AND CLASSIFICATION

162. **Definition.** When a proposition is introduced into an assembly, it is called a motion; when it is stated by the chair for the assembly to adopt or to reject, it is termed a question; but after adoption it is known as the order, the resolution, or the vote of the assembly.

163. **Classification.** There are five general classifications of motions:

(1) Main
(2) Incidental Main
(3) Subsidiary
(4) Incidental
(5) Privileged.

There are several matters which an assembly considers that are not introduced by a motion. These are more correctly termed questions. They are:

(1) Objection to the consideration of the question. (Section 230, p. 248.)

(2) Questions of privilege. (Section 221, p. 237.)

(3) Questions of order. (Section 228, p. 244.)

164. Relation of the Five Classifications of Motions.
Main motions may be adopted or rejected as offered;
however, some other action is usually taken. When a
main motion is introduced, the assembly may wish to
refer it to a committee for investigation and information,
or it may wish to lay the motion on the table until further
information can be secured, or it may wish to postpone
it to a certain time when some member who is well informed on the subject will be present. The assembly
may judge the matter not to be for the best interests of
the organization, in which case objection to the consideration of the question could be made. All classifications of motions are interrelated and necessary, one
to the other. The effect of one on another will be discussed in detail under the separate classifications.

165. Main Motions. A main motion is one which is
made to bring an independent proposition before the assembly. It cannot be made while any other proposition
is pending. There are two classifications of main motions. They are general and incidental.

(1) **General Main Motions** are motions which introduce some new proposition to the assembly. They are
subject to all motions and questions in the order of their
precedence. (Section 171, p. 177.)

(2) **Incidental Main Motions** are motions that apply
to methods of transacting business and matters of procedure rather than to business itself. The only difference between main motions and incidental main
motions is that objection to the consideration of the
question cannot be made to an incidental main motion.

They are in order whenever a main motion is in order, that is, when no other proposition is before the assembly. The making of the motion to reconsider and spread on the minutes and the motion to reconsider can interrupt other business. (Section 178, p. 183 & Section 179, p. 184.)

The following list of incidental main motions contains the ones most often used:

(1) Fix the method of making nominations when no election is pending. (Section 172, p. 178.)

(2) Fix method of voting when no other proposition is pending. (Section 173, p. 179.)

(3) Adjourn when qualified. (Section 174, p. 180.)

(4) Adjourn when adjournment would dissolve the assembly. (Section 175, p. 180.)

(5) Select a time and place for another meeting if introduced when there is nothing else before the assembly (fix time to which to adjourn when not privileged). (Section 176, p. 181.)

(6) Rescind. (Section 177, p. 182.)

(7) Reconsider and spread on the minutes. (Section 178, p. 183.)

(8) Reconsider. (Section 179, p. 184.)

(9) Amend the existing constitution, by-laws, or rules of order. (Section 180, p. 191.)

(10) Take from the table. (Section 181, p. 192.)

(11) Call of the house. (Section 182, p. 194.)

(12) Make a special order. (Section 184, p. 195.)

(13) Ratify. (Section 185, p. 196.)

166. **Subsidiary Motions.** Subsidiary motions are motions which apply to the main motion. They are made for the purpose of disposing of the question to which they apply. Each subsidiary motion affects a main motion in a different way and when made takes precedence of the main motion. The motions to lay on the table, the previous question, and the motion to postpone indefinitely cannot be amended. The others may. All subsidiary motions require a majority for adoption except the motion for the previous question which requires a two-thirds vote. Subsidiary motions have a fixed rank among themselves. When one of them is the immediately pending question, every other subsidiary motion above it in rank is in order and every other subsidiary motion below it in rank is out of order.

The subsidiary motions are listed here in the order of their rank beginning with the highest.

(1) Lay on the table. (Section 186, p. 200.)

(2) Previous question. (Section 187, p. 203.)

(3) Postpone to a certain time. (Section 194, p. 209.)

(4) Commit, refer, or recommit. (Section 196, p. 214.)

(5) Amend. (Section 202, p. 218.)

(6) Postpone indefinitely. (Section 216, p. 230.)

167. **Incidental Motions.** Incidental motions are those motions which arise out of pending questions. They take precedence of and must be disposed of before the questions out of which they arose can be decided. They yield to privileged questions and generally

to the motion to lay on the table. They are undebatable except an appeal under certain circumstances. (Section 229, p. 246.) No subsidiary motion except the motion to amend can be applied to any of them except a debatable appeal. It is often stated that all incidental motions take precedence of a certain motion. This is true when the motions are legitimately incidental to the motion of which they take precedence.

The incidental motions are listed as follows:

(1) Questions of order. (Section 228, p. 244.)

(2) Appeal. (Section 229, p. 246.)

(3) Objection to the consideration of the question. (Section 230, p. 248.)

(4) The reading of papers. (Section 231, p. 249.)

(5) Withdrawal of a motion. (Section 232, p. 250.)

(6) Suspension of rules. (Section 233, p. 251.)

(7) Limit or close debate. (Section 234, p. 252.)

(8) Extend the limits of debate. (Section 235, p. 254.)

(9) Approval or correction of the minutes. (Section 236, p. 255.)

(10) Fix method of voting when a proposition is pending. (Section 237, p. 256.)

(11) Fix method of making nominations when an election is pending. (Section 238, p. 256.)

(12) Continue speaking after indecorum. (Section 239, p. 257.)

(13) Close, open, and re-open nominations. (Section 119, p. 146 & Section 240, p. 258.)

(14) Set as a special order. (Section 241, p. 259.)

(15) Division of a question. (Section 242, p. 260.)

168. Privileged Motions and Questions of Privilege.
Privileged motions are motions of such importance that while they need not be related to the pending question, they take precedence of the pending question and all other questions. They relate to a future meeting of the organization, an adjournment, an intermission, or to questions concerning the honor and dignity of the organization as a whole or to a member in his official capacity, and to the authorized orders of the day. Because of their privilege, the raising of these privileged motions is undebatable. No subsidiary motions may be applied to these motions except the motion to amend, which may be applied to the motion to fix the time to which to adjourn and the motion to recess.

The privileged motions and questions of privilege are listed here in the order of their rank:

(1) Fix the time to which to adjourn. (Section 218, p. 233.)

(2) Adjourn. (Section 219, p. 234.)

(3) Take a recess. (Section 220, p. 236.)

(4) Questions of privilege: General privilege. (Section 221, p. 237.)

(5) Questions of privilege: Personal privilege (Section 223, p. 239.)

(6) Call for orders of the day. (Section 225, p. 241.)

RELATION TO ORGANIC LAW

169. Organic Law Controls. No motion or proposition is in order that is in conflict with the constitution, by-laws, rules of order or standing rules. If such a motion were made and adopted, it would be null and void. If the organic law of an organization prohibits some policy that the organization wishes to follow, amendments to the organic law should be adopted before a motion to adopt such a policy is introduced. Likewise no resolution or proposition can be adopted that is in conflict with one already adopted.

RANK OF MOTIONS

170. (A) Precedence. By precedence is meant the order of the rank of motions.

While a motion is being considered, one of higher rank which takes precedence of it can be made and must be disposed of before the motion of lower rank can be considered again.

Sometimes four or five motions, each of higher rank than the one before, can be pending at one time. It is like building a staircase. The first step is a main motion. Next a motion of higher rank is made, then another of still higher rank and so on up the staircase.

6.   Adjourn
5.   Lay on table
4.   Postpone to a certain time
3.   Commit
2.   Postpone indefinitely
1.   Main motion or resolution

The first motion to be voted on will be "to adjourn." If this is adopted, the other motions will not be considered at this time. If it is not adopted, the vote will be next on the motion of lower rank (the next step down), and so on down the staircase until a motion is adopted which disposes of the question, or until the main motion is reached.

(B) Yield. Yield, as it is used in the parliamentary sense, means "giving way to in time of consideration." Therefore motions of lower rank are said to yield to motions of higher rank.

STUDY AND DISCUSSION TOPICS

1. Name the five classes of motions. Define each.

2. Explain precedence or rank, giving an example.

3. What motions cannot be made before a main motion?

4. What is the relation of the five classes of motions, one to the other?

CHAPTER X.

MAIN MOTIONS

MAIN MOTIONS IN GENERAL

171. Main Motions.

Rank: A main motion cannot be made while any other proposition is before the assembly. The maker must obtain recognition. Main motions must be seconded.

Purpose: To bring some independent proposition before the assembly for the assembly to act upon.

Effect: The making of the motion brings the proposition before the assembly.   If the motion is adopted, the assembly takes the action proposed in the motion.

Form: "I move that—(here he states the nature of the action that he wishes the assembly to take)."

Yields: To all subsidiary, privileged, and incidental motions and is subject to them in the order of their precedence. (Section 170, p. 175.)

Precedence: Takes precedence of nothing.

Debatable: Yes.

Motions Applicable: All subsidiary motions may be applied. Objection to the consideration may be made. The vote may be reconsidered.

Adoption: Main motions require a majority vote.

INCIDENTAL MAIN MOTIONS

172. Fix Method of Making Nominations When No Election Is Pending.

Rank: This is an incidental main motion when no election is pending. (See Section 238, p. 256 for rank when an election is pending.) The maker must obtain recognition. The motion requires a second.

Purpose: To fix method to be used in making nominations.

Effect: Adoption of this motion fixes the method named as the one to be used.

Form: "I move that the nominations for permanent officers of this society be made by a nominating committee appointed by the chairman."

Yields: To all subsidiary, incidental, and privileged motions.

Precedence: Takes precedence of nothing.

Debatable: Yes.

Motions Applicable: All subsidiary motions may be applied. The vote may be reconsidered if no nomination has been made under the method adopted. Objection to the consideration of the question cannot be made.

Adoption: Majority vote is sufficient.

173. Fix Method of Voting When No Other Proposition Is Pending.

Rank: This is an incidental main motion if it does not refer to the vote to be taken on a specific proposition which is before the assembly. (See Section 237, p. 256 for rank of motion when it refers to the method of taking a vote on a pending proposition.) The maker must obtain recognition. The motion requires a second.

Purpose: To fix method to be used in voting.

Effect: Adoption of this motion fixes the method of voting to be used.

Form: "I move that this organization vote by ballot on expulsion of members."

Yields: To all subsidiary, incidental, and privileged motions.

Precedence: It takes precedence of nothing.

Debatable: Yes.

Motions Applicable: All subsidiary motions may be applied. The vote may be reconsidered if no action has been taken as a result of the vote. An objection to the consideration of the question may not be made.

Adoption: Majority vote is sufficient for adoption.

174. Adjourn When Qualified.

Rank: The motion to adjourn to a certain time has no privilege. It is an incidental main motion. It cannot interrupt a pending question. The maker must obtain recognition. The motion requires a second.

Purpose: To adjourn the assembly to some definite time.

Effect: The adoption of this motion forces the chair to declare the meeting adjourned until the time set for reassembling and provides an adjourned meeting.

Form: "I move that the assembly stand adjourned until one o'clock p.m. tomorrow."

Yields: To all subsidiary, privileged, and incidental motions.

Precedence: Takes precedence of nothing.

Debatable: Yes.

Motions Applicable: All subsidiary motions may be applied to it. Objection to the consideration may not be made. The motion to adjourn may be renewed after business has been transacted. A negative vote on a motion to adjourn cannot be reconsidered.

Adoption: A majority vote is sufficient for adoption.

175. Adjourn When the Adjournment Would Dissolve the Assembly.

Rank: This is an incidental main motion. It cannot interrupt a pending question. The maker of the motion must obtain recognition.   The motion must be seconded.

Purpose: To adjourn the assembly *sine die.*

Effect: If this motion is adopted, the meeting will be dissolved.

Form: "I move that the meeting stand adjourned."

Yields: To all subsidiary, privileged, and incidental motions.

Precedence: Takes precedence of nothing.

Debatable: Yes.

Motions Applicable: This motion is subject to all subsidiary motions in the order of their precedence. Objection to the consideration may not be made.   The motion may not be reconsidered but may be renewed after progress in consideration or debate.

Adoption: Majority vote is sufficient for adoption.

176. Fix the Time to Which to Adjourn (When Not Privileged).

Rank: This is an incidental main motion if made when no other question is before the assembly or when no provision has been made for another meeting.   (See Section 218, p. 233 for rank of motion if made when another proposition is pending.)   The maker must obtain recognition.   The motion requires a second.

Purpose: To fix the time and place of the next meeting or to provide an adjourned meeting.

Effect: Adoption of this motion provides the time and place for another meeting.

Form: "I move that when we adjourn, we adjourn to nine o'clock a. m., Saturday."

Yields: To all subsidiary, incidental and privileged motions.

Precedence: Takes precedence of nothing.

Debatable: Yes.

Motions Applicable: All subsidiary motions may be applied. An affirmative vote on the motion may be reconsidered. Objection to the consideration may not be made.

Adoption: Majority vote is sufficient for adoption.

177. Rescind.

Rank: This is an incidental main motion. It is in order when there is nothing else before the assembly. It cannot be made if the motion to reconsider can be made or a motion to reconsider, that has been made previously, can be called up. A motion to rescind cannot be made if the vote has caused something to be done that the assembly cannot undo. A motion to rescind a vote on a matter which authorized the making of a contract cannot be made if the other contracting party has been informed of the act. Notice of the motion to rescind may be given while another proposition is pending, but it cannot interrupt a speaker. The motion requires a second. The maker must obtain recognition.

Purpose: To repeal or annul some motion formerly adopted by the assembly, when the time element prevents a reconsideration.

Effect: The motion to rescind, if adopted, has the effect of an amendment which strikes out the motion formerly adopted.

Form: "I move to rescind the action of the assembly on — (here state the nature of the proposition)."

Yields: To all privileged, incidental and subsidiary motions.

Precedence: It takes precedence of nothing.

Debatable: It opens the merits of the main question to debate.

Motions Applicable: All subsidiary motions can be applied to it. An affirmative vote on the motion to rescind cannot be reconsidered. An objection to the consideration of the question cannot be raised.

Adoption: The motion to rescind, if notice has been given, may be adopted by a majority vote. If notice has not been given, either a two-thirds vote or a majority vote of the entire membership is necessary for adoption.

178. **Reconsider and Have Spread on the Minutes.**

Rank: This is an incidental main motion. The making of the motion has high privilege, interrupting any other business, even a speaker. It has higher rank than the simple motion to reconsider and can be made after the motion to reconsider has been voted on, if the vote has not yet been announced. The motion to reconsider and have spread on the minutes cannot be called up on the same day it is made unless it is made on the last day of the session. It can be made only on the day when the proposition sought to be reconsidered was voted on. It can apply only to those votes which finally dispose of a proposition, as the adoption or rejection of a main motion, an affirmative

vote on the motion to postpone indefinitely, and a
negative vote on the motion, "Will the assembly consider the proposition?" which is the way of stating the
question when an objection is made to the consideration
of a question.

Purpose: The difference between the simple motion
to reconsider and the motion to reconsider and have
spread on the minutes is that the simple motion to reconsider allows an organization to correct on the same
or the next day errors which may have been made, due
to lack of information; while the motion to reconsider
and have spread on the minutes prevents a temporary
majority from taking final action on a proposition which
would be contrary to the wishes of the actual majority.

Effect of Making the Motion: The making of the
motion holds in abeyance any action on the proposition
to which it applies until the motion is called up at some
other meeting.   If a motion to reconsider and have
spread on the minutes is not called up at the session
in which it was made, its effect ends with the session.

Effect of Calling Up the Motion: When this motion is called up it becomes a simple motion to reconsider and all the rules concerning the calling up of a
motion to reconsider (Section 179, p. 184) apply to it.

Form: "I move to reconsider the vote on the resolution concerning a book fair and have it spread on the
minutes."

179. Reconsider.

Rank: This is an incidental main motion.   The
making of the motion to reconsider has a higher privi-

lege than the consideration of the motion after it is made. It can be made only on the same day that the vote sought to be reconsidered was taken or on the next succeeding day. A recess or a legal holiday is not considered as a day. It must be made by one who voted on the prevailing side.*

The motion to reconsider can be made while any other question is pending except the motion to reconsider and have spread on the minutes (Section 178, p. 183.) It may even interrupt a member who has the floor. It may be made after the assembly has voted to adjourn but before the chair has announced the result of the vote. If it is made after the previous question has been ordered, both the motion to reconsider and the question to be reconsidered are undebatable.

A motion to reconsider, which was made previously, can be called up when general orders are being considered, if no question is pending.

While a main motion is being considered, a motion to reconsider the vote on another main motion can be made, although it cannot be considered at that time. The presiding officer instructs the secretary to make a note of the motion to reconsider. Then as soon as the main motion is disposed of or at a later time, a member can call up the motion to reconsider.

When several secondary motions are pending and a motion to reconsider the vote on one secondary motion is made, the chair automatically puts the question on the motion to reconsider as soon as the motion sought

---

*If a motion is adopted, the "ayes" are the prevailing side; if a motion is rejected, the "noes" are the prevailing side.

to be reconsidered would be in order. However, when a motion to reconsider a main motion is made but not disposed of, the chair does not put the question on the motion to reconsider the vote on the main motion until it is called up by some member.

The motion to reconsider can be made applying to any main motion unless:

(1) Some action has been taken as a result of the vote which is sought to be reconsidered;

(2) Previous notice was required for consideration of the proposition on which the vote is to be reconsidered;

(3) The vote was on a nomination or an election and the candidate has been notified of his nomination or election;

(4) The vote was an affirmative one on a contract and the other party has been notified of the vote; or

(5) The vote was on a motion referring a proposition to a committee and the committee has commenced work on the proposition.*

The motion to reconsider cannot apply to the vote on a motion that may be renewed within a reasonable length of time, except in the case of a motion to limit debate. A motion to reconsider the vote on a motion to limit debate is in order even after debate has taken place under the motion to limit.

The motion to reconsider cannot be made to apply to votes on the following motions:

---

*After a committee has commenced work on a proposition referred to it, the only way the proposition can be removed from the committee is by a motion that the committee be discharged from the consideration of the proposition. (See Section 79, page 125.)

(1) To adjourn

(2) To take a recess

(3) To lay on the table

(4) To take from the table

(5) To suspend the rules or the regular order of business

(6) To reconsider*

(7) An affirmative vote on call for orders of the day

(8) An affirmative vote on adoption of a constitution, by-laws, rules of order, or standing rules

(9) An affirmative vote on amending any rule that requires previous notice for its amendment

(10) An affirmative vote reopening nominations

(11) A negative vote on a motion to postpone indefinitely.

Purpose: To reopen a question already voted on or to hold in abeyance final action on a matter.

Effect of Making the Motion: A motion to reconsider holds in abeyance any action that would be taken as a result of the vote sought to be reconsidered.

Effect of the Adoption of the Motion: The adoption of the motion to reconsider cancels the vote previously taken on the proposition and places it before the assembly again in the same position it had before it was voted upon. If the motion to reconsider is made and adopted on the same day that the vote to be reconsidered was taken, no one who had used his time in debate can speak again on the adoption of the

---

*A second motion to reconsider cannot be made on the same proposition unless the proposition was materially changed when it was reconsidered the first time.

question. He could, of course, speak on the motion to reconsider. If, however, the motion to reconsider a vote is made but not acted upon on the same day that the vote was taken, debate is free.

If the vote sought to be reconsidered was taken under the operation of the previous question and the previous question was exhausted with the taking of that vote, the motion is open to debate on reconsideration and, if the reconsideration carries, on the adoption of the question. If the motion to reconsider is made on a vote when the previous question is still pending, the motion to reconsider and the proposition reconsidered are undebatable.

Form: When a Main Proposition is to be Reconsidered: "I move to reconsider the vote by which the resolution that the club hold a book fair was adopted (or rejected)."

When a Secondary Motion to a Pending Proposition is to be Reconsidered: "I move to reconsider the vote by which the amendment to the pending resolution, adding the words, 'on June 1' was adopted (or rejected)."

When a Secondary Motion to a Proposition Already Adopted is to be Reconsidered: "I move to reconsider the votes on the resolution that the club hold a book fair and on the amendment adding the words 'on June 1'."

Yields: The making of the motion yields to no other business except a motion to reconsider and have spread on the minutes. If a motion to reconsider is pending when a motion to reconsider and spread on the minutes is made, the motion to reconsider is ignored as if it had never been made. The consideration of the motion to reconsider yields to those motions to which the motion sought to be reconsidered would yield.

Precedence: The making of the motion to reconsider takes precedence of everything except the making of the motion to reconsider and spread on the minutes. It can be made while another proposition is pending or it may even interrupt a speaker. When the motion for reconsideration is called up, it takes the rank of the motion sought to be reconsidered, taking precedence of a new motion of that same rank.

Debatable: It is debatable only when the question to be reconsidered is debatable.

Motions Applicable: The motion to reconsider cannot be amended, committed, or postponed indefinitely. The motion for the previous question can apply to the motion to reconsider when it is debatable. The motion to lay on the table and the motion to postpone to a certain time can be made applying to a motion to reconsider. If the motion to table carries, the proposition sought to be reconsidered goes to the table also. If the motion to postpone to a certain time is adopted, the proposition sought to be reconsidered adheres to the motion to reconsider. The motion to reconsider cannot be withdrawn after it is too late to renew the motion. If a motion to reconsider is made and lost, it cannot be renewed unless general consent is given.

Reconsidering Secondary Motions to a Pending Proposition: If a motion to reconsider the vote on a secondary motion is made when it can be taken up, that is, when no motion of higher rank is immediately pending, the chair puts the question on the motion to reconsider immediately. If a motion to reconsider the vote on a secondary motion is made but cannot be considered at once because other motions of higher rank are pending and must be disposed of first, the chair automatically puts the question on the motion to reconsider as soon as the motion sought to be reconsidered would be in order.

Example: A main motion is pending. A motion to commit is made and fails of adoption. A motion to postpone to a certain time and a motion to lay on the table are made. Then someone moves to reconsider the vote by which the motion to commit failed of adoption. The question is not put on the reconsideration until the motion to commit is in order. Instead the motion to lay on the table is voted on. If it fails of adoption, the motion to postpone to a certain time is voted on. If this also fails, the question is put on reconsideration of the motion to commit. Had the main proposition been either laid on the table or postponed, the motion to reconsider the motion to commit would have gone with the main motion and been pending when the proposition was again considered.

Reconsidering Amendments to a Main Motion Already Adopted: If after a main motion as amended is adopted, it becomes necessary to reconsider the vote on any primary or secondary amendment or both, the motion to reconsider must include all the votes sought to be reconsidered.

For example: "Mr. President, I move to reconsider the votes on the resolution relating to the book fair and on the amendment to it." Or, "I move to reconsider the votes on the resolution, the amendment, and the amendment to the amendment which related to the book fair."

If the motion to reconsider includes more than one question, debate is limited to the question first voted on. In the case of the main motion, the amendment and the amendment to the amendment, debate would be limited to the amendment to the amendment as it was first voted on.

After the motion to reconsider is adopted, the presiding officer recognizes the maker of the motion to reconsider as having the right to first debate. After a reconsideration, motions included in the motion to reconsider are in exactly the same position they were before the vote on adoption. They can be amended, debated or have any of the subsidiary motions applied to them.

180. **Amend the Existing Constitution, By-laws, or Rules of Order.**

Rank: This is an incidental main motion. It is the motion used when a member wishes to offer an amendment to the organic law. The maker must obtain recognition. The motion requires a second.

Purpose: To make a change in the instrument sought to be amended.

Effect: If the motion is adopted, the change is made.

Form: "I move to amend the constitution—(here state the nature of the amendment)."

Yields: A motion to amend any of these three instruments yields to all subsidiary motions, privileged motions and incidental motions except the objection to the consideration of the question.

Precedence: It takes precedence of nothing.

Debatable: Yes.

Motions Applicable: All of the subsidiary motions except the motion to postpone indefinitely can apply to the motion to amend the instruments of organic law.

Adoption: The instrument sought to be amended should provide the terms of its own amendment. As a rule, they require that they shall be amended by amendments of which previous notice has been given and that the amendments be adopted by a two-thirds vote. While a proposed amendment to any of the instruments of organic law is pending, an incidental motion may be adopted setting the time at which the amendment shall become effective. If this is not done, the amendment, if adopted, goes into effect immediately. The incidental motion to set the time at which the proposed amendment shall become effective is adopted by a majority vote.

181. Take From the Table.

Rank: This is an incidental main motion. It does not take precedence of a pending motion, but when no question is immediately pending, the motion to take from the table takes precedence of a new main motion.

The motion to take from the table can be made only during the same session that laid the proposition on the table. The maker must obtain recognition. It requires a second.

When a member rises to make a motion to take from the table and the chair recognizes another, the member should say, "Mr. Chairman, I rise to make a motion to take from the table." If the person whom the chair had previously recognized has risen for the purpose of making a new main motion, the chair should give the floor to the member who wishes to make a motion to take from the table. If, however, the person recognized by the chair has already made a new motion and the chair has stated it, the member wishing to make the motion to take from the table must wait until the new question is disposed of.

It is not in order to make a motion to take from the table unless some business has been transacted since the proposition was laid on the table. The motion to reconsider cannot apply to a negative vote on the motion to take from the table because the motion to take from the table, if lost, can be repeated after some business has been transacted. An affirmative vote on the motion to take from the table cannot be reconsidered because the motion to lay on the table can be made again.

Purpose: To bring up for consideration some proposition that has been laid on the table earlier in the session.

Effect: If the motion to take from the table is adopted, the proposition comes from the table exactly as it went to the table. If a resolution is laid on the table with an amendment pending, the amendment will be considered when the resolution is taken up. If a motion to commit is pending when the proposition goes to the table the motion to commit will be considered when the resolution is taken from the table. If, however, a motion to postpone to a certain time is pending when the proposition is laid on the table, and the day to which the motion sought to postpone the proposition has passed, the motion to postpone is not considered.

When a proposition is taken from the table on the same day that it was laid on the table, those who have spoken on the proposition cannot speak again; but if taken from the table on a different day, debate begins anew.

Form: "I move that the proposition (here state the nature of the proposition) be taken from the table."

Yields: This motion yields to privileged and incidental motions.

Precedence: It takes precedence of new main motions. It is in order when unfinished business or new business may be considered.

Debatable: No.

Motions Applicable: Subsidiary motions cannot be applied to this motion. Objection to the consideration may not be made.

Adoption: A majority vote is required for adoption.

182. **Call of the House.** Call of the house is not applicable in many organizations. Its object is to compel the attendance of the absent members who are unexcused. It may also be made to include the members who have been excused. When the absence of a quorum is noted,

a call of the house is in order. This motion must pass by a majority of the members present. After a call is ordered, the assembly must await the arrival of a quorum before it can transact any business, or if the sergeant-at-arms reports the likelihood of getting a quorum is doubtful, the assembly may adjourn.

Rank of Motion: The motion for a call of the house is a motion of general privilege when there is no quorum. It can take precedence of minutes or the journal. It yields only to a motion to adjourn. When a quorum is present and a motion for a call of the house is made, it is treated as any other main motion.

183. **Procedure under a Call of the House.** When a call is ordered, the clerk calls the roll and notes the absentees who are absent without excuses. The clerk gives the names of the unexcused absent members to the sergeant-at-arms who is directed by the presiding officer to find the absent members and bring them to the house. A list of the persons sought to be brought before the house is handed to the sergeant-at-arms with the signature of the presiding officer, attested by the clerk and the secretary. Elective bodies usually adopt such a rule as the call of the house in order that they may compel the attendance of the members to transact the business before the assembly.

184. **To Set as a Special Order when an Incidental Main Motion.**

Rank: If a motion to set a proposition as a special order is made when no other proposition is before the assembly, it is an incidental main motion.

Purpose: To insure special consideration of the proposition sought to be set as a special order.

Effect: The motion to set as a special order, if carried, suspends all the rules which interfere with the consideration of the proposition at the time set.

Form: "I move that the resolution (here state the nature of the resolution) be set as a special order for Thursday morning at 11 o'clock.

Yields: It yields to all incidental and privileged motions. It also yields to all subsidiary motions which apply to it as to a main motion.

Precedence: This motion takes precedence of nothing. It is in order when a main motion would be in order.

Debatable: Yes.

Motions Applicable: All subsidiary motions apply because it is an incidental main motion. A motion to reconsider may apply to an affirmative vote on a special order, but not to a negative vote for the reason that this motion may be renewed.

Adoption: This motion requires a two-thirds vote.

185. **Ratify.**

Rank: This is an incidental main motion. It is used when an organization must confirm or concur in some action taken by its executive committee or some other committee to whom it had delegated authority. It is also used when an organization desires to accept the action of some other body as its action. For instance, an amendment to the Constitution of the United States is submitted by the Federal Congress to the various state legislatures for ratification. The state legislatures cannot amend the proposed amendment in any way. They can only ratify or reject.

The maker of the motion must obtain recognition. A second is required.

Purpose: The distinction between the purpose of the motion to adopt and that of the motion to ratify may be made in this manner: The motion to adopt is used to apply to an original proposition. The motion to ratify is used when an organization wishes to concur in or confirm the action of a group acting in a certain relation to that organization.

Effect: The motion to ratify, if adopted, makes the action of some other body the action of the assembly. The motion cannot validate an invalid action of the assembly. The only exception is that a quorum may ratify some action taken in an emergency by a group less than a quorum. If a committee or an individual takes certain action without authority, the organization may ratify the action or it may censure the action as it sees fit.

Form: "I move to ratify the statement of objectives recently proposed by our national organization."

Yields: To all privileged motions and motions incidental to itself.

Precedence: It takes precedence of nothing.

Debatable: The motion to ratify is debatable and opens the entire question to debate.

Motions Applicable: The proposition sought to be ratified cannot be amended if the proposition is submitted by the parent group to a branch organization for ratification.

For Example: If the Federal Congress submits a constitutional amendment to the legislatures of the various states for ratification, the state legislatures cannot amend the proposition submitted. They can only ratify or reject.

The motion to ratify may be amended under these circumstances: If the motion to ratify is made for the purpose of validating some action taken by an individual or a group of persons within the organization, the motion may be amended by substituting a motion to censure.

The motion for the previous question can be applied to the motion to ratify. The motions to lay on the table, to postpone to a certain time, and to postpone indefinitely can be applied also. The vote can be reconsidered if notification has not been made. Objection to the consideration of the question cannot be raised.

Adoption: The vote required for adoption is a majority vote unless some other vote is specified in the rules of that particular organization.

STUDY AND DISCUSSION TOPICS

1. Of what motions do main motions take precedence?

2. Give examples of the motion to fix the method of making nominations when no election is pending and the motion to fix method of voting when no other proposition is pending, and tell what vote is required for adoption of each.

3. Explain the difference between rescind and reconsider.

4. How may a constitution be amended?

5. When may the motion to take from the table be made?

6. In what organizations is call of the house used? When is it in order?

7. Give an example of a motion to set as a special order. What vote does it require?

8. What is a proper subject for a main motion to introduce?

9. How many main motions can be pending at one time?

10. If a motion is defeated, can it come up for consideration again? How can this be done?

CHAPTER XI.

SUBSIDIARY MOTIONS

LAY ON THE TABLE

186. **Rank:** The motion to lay on the table is first in rank of the six subsidiary motions. The maker must obtain recognition. The motion must be seconded. It may be applied to:

(1) Any main motion.

(2) Any question of privilege or question of order after it is before the assembly for consideration.

(3) An appeal from the ruling of the chair when the reversal of the ruling would not affect the main question.

(4) A motion to reconsider. If the motion to table a motion to reconsider carries, the proposition sought to be reconsidered goes to the table with the motion to reconsider.

The motion to table can be made at any time during debate before the final voting on a proposition begins. Even after the previous question has been ordered on a series of motions and the vote has been taken on one or more of the pending motions under the previous question, the motion to table may be made. If the motion to table carries while the previous question is in effect, when the proposition comes from the table the previous question will still be in effect.

The motion to table cannot be applied to any proposition which is not the pending question. A series of resolutions or a number of committee reports cannot be laid on the table at one time. However, a series of propositions may be laid on the table in this manner. As each proposition is taken up, a member may move that the proposition be laid on the table until the entire series of resolutions has been laid on the table.

If a proposition is taken from the table, it is not in order to move to lay it on the table on the same day unless there is a definite change in the proposition.

If a question of privilege is laid on the table, the question which was interrupted by the question of privilege is not affected.

Purpose: The purpose of this motion is to delay consideration and decision on a question. It is often used to dispose of propositions temporarily so that some other proposition can be taken up. This motion is used sometimes as a method of disposing of a measure. While it is effective as a method of disposing of a proposition temporarily, it must be remembered that a majority can take the proposition from the table.

Effect: The effect of the motion to table is to remove a proposition from the consideration of the assembly. As a rule, everything that adheres to a proposition goes to the table. When a motion is made to table a main motion, the pending amendments, if any, go to the table with the main motion. The following are exceptions to this rule:

(1) If an appeal from the decision of the chair is laid on the table, the action has the effect of confirming the chair's decision, at least while the appeal is on the table. The motion to lay the appeal on the table, if carried, would not carry the proposition upon which the appeal is made to the table with it unless a reversal of the ruling of the chair would keep the assembly from considering the proposition. (Section 229, p. 246.)

(2) A further exception is seen on the adoption of a motion to table an amendment to the minutes. The amendment would go to the table, but would not carry the minutes with it. The motion is, in this case, a method of refusing to amend the minutes without irrevocably refusing to amend. The amendment could be called from the table at any time by a majority vote.

If a motion to table an amendment to a proposition already adopted, such as the constitution or by-laws, carries, it does not carry the constitution or by-laws with it.

Form: "I move to lay the question on the table."

This motion must not be qualified in any way. "To lay the question on the table until four o'clock p. m." is not a proper motion. The motion to postpone to a certain time should be made instead.

Yields: It yields to privileged motions and motions incidental to itself.

Precedence: Takes precedence of the other subsidiary motions which are of lower rank and any incidental motions that may be pending.

Debatable: No.

Motions Applicable: No other subsidiary motion can be applied to it. The motion to reconsider does not apply to this motion because:

(1) An affirmative vote can be reversed by making a motion to take from the table (this requires the same vote as to lay on the table).

(2) A negative vote can be reversed by renewing the motion (making it again) after progress in debate.

Adoption: A majority vote is sufficient for adoption.

THE PREVIOUS QUESTION

187. **Rank.** The previous question is second in rank of the subsidiary motions. The maker must obtain recognition. It requires a second. It takes precedence of all subsidiary motions except the motion to lay on the table. After the previous question has been ordered on a series of questions and the vote has not been taken on all the questions included in the previous question, the motion to table may be made and applied to the questions not yet voted on. If a proposition goes to the table, the previous question is not exhausted but is still in effect when the proposition is taken from the table.

Purpose: To bring the immediately pending question or series of pending questions to a vote.

Effect: The effect of the motion for the previous

question, if adopted, is to close debate instantly on the question or questions included in the motion.

If the motion for the previous question includes more than one question, the effect of the previous question lasts until all of the questions included are disposed of. (See Section 190, p. 206.)

If the previous question fails to carry, discussion continues as though the motion had never been made.

Form: There are two forms of moving the previous question. The correct form depends upon the purpose of the motion. If the purpose is to bring the immediately pending question to a vote, the form is: "I move the previous question."

If the purpose is to move the previous question on a series of pending motions, the form is: "I move the previous question on (here list the motions)." The previous question applies to the series of motions in consecutive order beginning with the immediately pending motion.

Example of previous question applying to immediately pending motion: If a main motion and an amendment are pending and someone moves the previous question by saying: "I move the previous question," the amendment alone is included. If the previous question is adopted, debate is cut off and the amendment is put to the vote immediately. After this vote is taken, the main question is open to debate and subsidiary motions.

Example of previous question applying to a series of motions: If a main motion, a motion to amend, and a motion to commit are pending and someone moves the previous question in this manner, "I move the previous question on the motion to commit, the motion to amend, and the main motion," all three motions are included. If the previous question is adopted, debate is cut off and the vote is taken on the motions in their consecutive order beginning with the immediately pending one, in this case, the motion to commit.

Yields: The motion for the previous question yields to all privileged and incidental motions and to the motion to lay on the table.

Precedence: It takes precedence of and applies to all debatable motions. It takes precedence of all subsidiary motions except the motion to lay on the table.

Debatable: No.

188. **Motions Applicable.** It cannot have any subsidiary motion applied to it. However, the effect of an amendment to a pending motion for the previous question may be achieved by moving the previous question on more motions than were included in the original motion for the previous question. This is treated as amendment by substituting. (See Section 213, p. 228.)

Example: If a main motion, a motion to amend, and a motion to commit are pending, and a member moves the previous question on the motion to commit by saying: "I move the previous question," another member may offer a second motion for the previous question by saying, "I move the previous question on the motion to commit, the motion to amend, and the main motion." This second motion is treated as a substitute for the first. The motion which orders the previous question on the largest number of questions is voted on first. If adopted, the question is put next on "the adoption of the motion as substituted." If the substitute motion fails, the question is on "the adoption of the motion for the previous question."

A motion to reconsider may apply to the motion for the previous question. (See Section 192, p. 207.)

Adoption: The adoption of the motion for the previous question requires a two-thirds vote, because it suspends the rule of free debate.

189. Reconsideration under the Previous Question.
If after the previous question has been ordered, a motion is made to reconsider a vote taken under the previous question, there can be no debate on the motion to reconsider although under other circumstances it would be debatable. Neither can the proposition reconsidered while the previous question is in force and effect be amended.

190. Exhaustion of the Previous Question.
The effect of the previous question is exhausted or terminated by the following circumstances:

(1) When the previous question is not qualified, its effect is terminated as soon as the immediately pending question to which it applies is voted on.

(2) If the previous question is ordered on a consecutive series of pending motions, its effect is terminated as soon as the last motion on which it was ordered is voted on, or when one motion already voted on commits the proposition or postpones it, either to a certain time or indefinitely.

191. Who May Speak After the Previous Question is Ordered. No one may speak in debate after the previous question is ordered. Several motions may be made while the previous question is in effect, as listed in Section 192, p. 207, but they are undebatable.

192. What May Be Considered after the Previous Question Has Been Ordered.

(1) The motion to reconsider the vote by which the assembly ordered the previous question may be made if no vote has been taken under the previous question. The motion to reconsider the previous question may be made only once.

(2) A motion for a call of the house and motions incidental to the call.

(3) Reconsideration of a vote taken under the previous question. (Section 189, p. 206.)

(4) Privileged motions* and questions of privilege.

(5) The motion to lay on the table.

(6) An appeal from the decision of the chair.**

193. Examples of Procedure Under the Previous Question.

(1) These motions are pending and the motion for the previous question includes all of them:

A main motion,

A motion to amend,

A motion to commit,

A motion to postpone to a certain time.

---

*When an assembly adjourns without a quorum while the previous question is in force, the previous question will still be in force when the proposition is taken up again.

**An appeal from the decision of the chair is always undebatable if made when the previous question is in force.

If the motion for the previous question carries, or is adopted, the chair immediately puts the question on the adoption of the motion to postpone to a certain time. If this motion carries, the motions to commit and to amend are postponed with the main motion. If, however, the motion to postpone to a certain time loses, the chair immediately puts the question on the motion to commit. If the motion to commit is adopted, the motion to amend and the main motion are committed, and the effect of the previous question is exhausted. If the motion to commit loses, the chair immediately puts the question on the motion to amend, and then on the adoption of either the main motion or the main motion as amended, as the case may be.

(2) The following motions are pending and the motion for the previous question is made to apply to the motion to postpone to a certain time only:

A main motion,
A motion to amend,
A motion to commit,
A motion to postpone to a certain time.

If the motion for the previous question is adopted, the chair puts the question on the adoption of the motion to postpone to a certain time. If the motion to postpone to a certain time is adopted, the other pending motions are postponed. If, however, the motion to postpone to a certain time is lost, the effect of the motion for the previous question is exhausted and debate continues on the other motions.

POSTPONE TO A CERTAIN TIME

194. **Rank.** This motion is third in rank of the subsidiary motions; it requires a second. The maker must obtain recognition.

Purpose: To postpone a proposition until a certain time, which must be within the limits of the current session. If the motion should postpone to a time the organization could not consider it, the motion would not be in order.

Effect: This motion, if adopted, postpones consideration of the proposition until the stated time and removes the proposition from the consideration of the assembly. The proposition then becomes a general order for the day named unless it is made a special order in the manner stated below. It cannot be considered before that time except by a reconsideration or by suspending the rules for that purpose.

Form: The form of the motion to postpone to a certain time depends upon the purpose of the maker. The following forms are listed according to purpose:

(1) If the purpose is to postpone consideration of the proposition until the next meeting, the form is "I move to postpone consideration of this proposition until the next regular meeting." The motion requires a majority vote to adopt. If the proposition is so postponed, it becomes a general order for the next meeting and will be considered before new business.

(2) If the purpose is to postpone consideration of the proposition until some scheduled business is disposed of, the form is: "I move to postpone considera-

tion of this measure until after the scheduled program."
This motion requires a majority vote to adopt. If so
postponed, the proposition becomes the pending business after the program is over.

(3) If the purpose of the motion is to set an hour at
which the proposition sought to be postponed will be
considered, the form is "I move to postpone consideration of the measure until 2:00 p. m. today."*

(4) If the consideration is of such importance that
it is desired to provide an adjourned meeting and de-
vote the entire meeting to the consideration of the
question, the form is: "I move to postpone consideration
of this proposition until next Friday afternoon." This
motion requires a majority vote for adoption. If a
motion is made to postpone consideration of a question
until an adjourned meeting, the time for the adjourned
meeting should be provided before the motion to postpone consideration of the proposition is voted on. This
may be done by making the incidental main motion that
"when we adjourn, we adjourn to 2:00 p. m. Friday."
If this motion to provide an adjourned meeting is
adopted, the chair puts the question on the motion to
postpone the consideration of the proposition until 2:00
p. m. Friday.

---

*The difference in effect between this motion to postpone to a cer-
tain hour and the motion to set as a special order for a certain hour
is this: When the time arrives for the consideration of a special order,
the presiding officer immediately puts the proposition before the
assembly for consideration regardless of what is pending business.
When the hour arrives for the consideration of a proposition which
was postponed to that hour, if no other proposition is pending, the
chair lays the proposition so postponed before the assembly. However,
should the assembly be engaged in considering another question, the
proposition postponed to that hour must wait until the pending business
is disposed of.

(5) If it is desired to amend the motion to postpone by making the consideration of the proposition a special order, the form is: "I move to amend the motion to postpone the proposition by adding the words, 'and make it a special order for 3:00 p. m. on our next regular meeting day.'" The adoption of the amendment requires a majority vote, but the adoption of the motion as amended, setting the proposition as a special order requires a two-thirds vote for adoption. (See Section 195, p. 212.)

Yields: It yields to the motion to lay on the table, the motion for the previous question, and all the privileged and incidental motions.

Precedence: It takes precedence of the motions to commit, to amend, and to postpone indefinitely.

Debatable: The motion to postpone to a certain time does not open the merits of the main question to debate, and for that reason debate should be limited to the propriety of the postponement.*

Motions Applicable: The motion to postpone to a certain time cannot be laid on the table, but a motion to lay the main proposition on the table can be made while the motion to postpone to a certain time is pending. If the main proposition is laid on the table, the motion to postpone to a certain time goes with it.

The motion for the previous question can be applied to the motion to postpone to a certain time.

The motion to postpone to a certain time can be amend-

---

*If an amendment making the proposition a special order is offered to the motion to postpone to a certain time, the amendment is not debatable, neither is the motion as amended. (See Section 195, p. 212.)

ed by changing the time or by offering an amendment to make the postponement a special order.

The motions to postpone indefinitely and to commit cannot be applied to the motion to postpone to a certain time.

The motion to reconsider can be applied to an affirmative vote on the motion to postpone to a certain time, but not to a negative one because the motion to postpone may be renewed later.

Adoption: The motion to postpone to a certain time requires a majority vote for adoption unless it has been amended to make the proposition a special order, in which case a two-thirds vote is necessary on the adoption of the motion as amended.

195. Special Order as an Amendment to Postpone to a Certain Time.

Rank: When the motion to postpone to a certain time is pending and an amendment which would make consideration of the proposition a special order is offered, it changes the status of the motion to postpone in this respect: the amendment to set as a special order is not debatable; the motion as amended is also undebatable and requires a two-thirds vote for adoption.

Purpose: To make a special order of the proposition sought to be postponed as a general order.

Effect: The adoption of the amendment and the motion as amended suspends all the rules which interfere with the consideration of the proposition.

Form: "I move to amend the motion to postpone to

a certain time by adding the words: 'and that it be made a special order for 11:00 a. m. Friday.' "

Yields: To all privileged and incidental motions and to the motion to lay on the table.

The motion to table may be made and acted on while the motion to postpone and the amendment to the motion to postpone are pending. If the motion to table prevails, the pending motions go with the main proposition to the table.

Precedence: This amendment to set as a special order takes precedence of any other amendment that might be offered.

Debatable: No. The rule is that a motion to set as a special order is debatable only when the proposition concerned is not before the assembly. In other words, of the three methods of setting a special order, only one motion is debatable, an incidental main motion. The incidental motion and the amendment to a motion to postpone to a certain time are both undebatable.

Motions Applicable: The amendment to set as a special order can be amended by changing the time. No other subsidiary motion can apply to the amendment. An affirmative vote on the motion to set as a special order can be reconsidered; a negative one cannot because the motion can be renewed.

Adoption: The amendment to the motion to postpone to a certain time, making the proposition a special order is adopted by a majority, but the adoption of the motion as amended requires a two-thirds vote.

COMMIT, REFER OR RECOMMIT

196. **Rank.** This motion is fourth in rank of the subsidiary motions. It requires a second. The maker must obtain recognition.

Purpose: The motion to commit is made to send a proposition to a committee for investigation, amendment, or other recommendation. The friends of a measure make the motion in order to send the proposition to a smaller group where it can be perfected. Sometimes they have the additional incentive that the favorable recommendation of a committee will have a greater influence with the organization than will the arguments of the proponents of the measure. The enemies of a motion may make the motion to commit as a means of delaying consideration. This is not a good motion for that purpose except as a last resort when more effective measures have failed to suppress it, or where the enemies of the measure feel that the investigations of a committee will reveal unfavorable aspects.

In a large organization where there is much business to be attended to, committees are used to weed out worthless propositions and to give closer consideration than is possible in assembly.

Effect: The motion to commit, when adopted, removes the proposition from the consideration of the assembly until the committee reports it, or until the assembly removes it from the committee.

If the motion to commit is adopted when a main proposition and a motion to postpone indefinitely are pending, the main proposition goes to the committee alone and the motion to postpone indefinitely is lost.

A motion to commit may be made applying to a main proposition to which one or two amendments are pending. If the motion to commit is adopted, the main proposition and any pending amendments go to the committee together. When the proposition is reported from committee the amendments will be pending.

197. **Form:** The wording of the motion depends upon the purpose of the maker. The motion to commit may take any of the following forms:

(1) That the resolution be referred to a committee;

(2) That the resolution be referred to a standing committee (here name the standing committee);

(3) That the resolution be referred to a special committee (here state the number on the special committee and the method of selection);

(4) That the resolution be referred to a special committee, without reference to the number on the committee or the method of selection;

(5) That the resolution be referred to a committee, either standing or special, with instructions (here state the nature of the instructions);

(6) That the organization resolve itself into a committee of the whole for the purpose of considering (here state the nature of the proposition);

(7) That the proposition be considered in quasi-committee of the whole;

(8) That the matter be considered informally.

Yields: This motion yields to the motion to lay on the table, the motion for the previous question, and the motion to postpone to a certain time. It yields also to all privileged and incidental motions.

Precedence: This motion takes precedence of the motions to amend and to postpone indefinitely.

Debatable: It opens debate to a limited extent on the propriety of committing the question.

Motions Applicable: The motion to commit can not be applied to any other subsidiary motion. The motion for the previous question and the motion to limit or extend debate may be applied to the motion to commit without affecting the main question.

The motion to commit cannot be postponed to a certain time nor can it be laid on the table, but the main motion can be postponed to a certain time or laid on the table while the motion to commit is pending. If this is done, the pending motion to commit goes with the main proposition. The motion to postpone indefinitely cannot be applied to the motion to commit. The motion to commit can be amended. (Section 198, p. 216.)

Adoption: A simple majority is required for adoption.

198. **How Amended.** There are five ways to amend the motion to commit:

(1) By adding the name of a committee to the motion to commit;

(2) By striking out the name of one committee and

inserting in lieu thereof the name of another committee;

(3) By giving certain instructions to the committee;

(4) By providing for the number of members to compose the committee, in the event the motion to commit provides for a special committee;

(5) By providing the method of selecting the personnel of the committee when the motion provides for the appointment of a special committee.

199. **Reconsider.** A motion to reconsider a motion to commit, refer, or recommit may be made if the motion to reconsider is made within the proper time limit (Section 179, p. 184) and before the committee has started to work on the proposition.

200. **Various Committees.** When various committees are proposed, they should be considered in the following order:

(1) Committee of the whole

(2) Quasi-committee of the whole

(3) Informal consideration

(4) Standing committee

(5) Special committee

If the proposition is referred to either the committee of the whole or to a standing committee, no specification as to the number of committeemen, time of meeting, or selection of a chairman is necessary. If the proposition is referred to a special committee, further provisions must be made as to the number of committeemen, time of meeting, selection of a chairman, time for report and other matters incidental thereto.

An assembly may discharge a committee from further consideration of a proposition. (Section 79, p. 125.)

201. **Recommit.** A matter which is sent back to the same or a different committee is recommitted.

AMEND

202. **Rank.** This motion is fifth in rank of subsidiary motions. It requires a second. The maker must obtain recognition. A motion to amend by filling blanks requires neither recognition nor second.

Purpose: To make a change in a pending proposition.

Effect: If the motion to amend is adopted, the proposition so amended is altered.

Yields: The motion to amend yields to all subsidiary motions except the motion to postpone indefinitely. It also yields to all privileged and incidental questions except the motion to divide the question.

Precedence: The motion to amend takes precedence of the proposition to which it applies and of the motion to postpone indefinitely.

Debatable: The motion to amend is debatable except when the proposition to which the amendment is offered is undebatable. When debatable, debate is restricted to the subject matter included in the amendment.

Motions Applicable: The motion for the previous question can be applied to the amendment alone when the amendment is debatable. The incidental motion to limit or extend the limits of debate can be made applying to the amendment alone. However, the motion for the previous question and the motion to limit or extend the limits of debate can be made to include the amendments and the main proposition, if the motion is so made. The motion to reconsider a vote on an amendment before the main motion is adopted can be made; likewise, a motion to reconsider an amendment to a main proposition already adopted can be made. (See Section 179, p. 184.) The motion to commit cannot apply to the amendment alone but may be made when an amendment is pending, and if the motion to commit is adopted, the amendment goes to the committee with the main proposition. The motion to table may be made while an amendment is pending, and if the motion to table carries, the amendment goes to the table with the main proposition. The motion to postpone indefinitely cannot be made against an amendment. The motion to postpone to a certain time can be made applying to the main proposition while the motion to amend is pending, and if the proposition is postponed, the pending amendment is postponed with it.

203. **Adoption.** An amendment to a pending proposition requires a simple majority for adoption even though the proposition to be amended requires a two-thirds vote on adoption. An amendment to the constitution or by-laws or rules of order already adopted is in reality an incidental main motion and requires a two-thirds vote. (See Section 180, p. 191.) However, an amendment to an amendment to the constitution, by-laws, or rules of order may be adopted by a majority vote if it is in order.

204. **Motions That Cannot Be Amended.**

(1) To adjourn (when privileged). (Section 219, p. 234.)

(2) Call for the orders of the day. (Section 225, p. 241.)

(3) Questions of order. (Section 228, p. 244.)

(4) Appeal. (Section 229, p. 246.)

(5) Objection to the consideration of a question. (Section 230, p.248.)

(6) The reading of papers. (Section 231, p. 249.)

(7) Leave to withdraw a motion. (Section 232, p. 250.)

(8) Suspension of the rules. (Section 233, p. 251.)

(9) Lay on the table. (Section 186, p. 200.)

(10) Previous question. (Section 187, p. 203.)

(11) An amendment to the amendment. (Section 205 p. 221.)

(12) Postpone indefinitely. (Section 216, p. 230.)

(13) Reconsider. (Section 179, p. 184.)

(14) Reconsider and have spread on the minutes. (Section 178, p. 183.)

(15) Take from the table. (Section 181, p. 192.)

(16) Leave to continue speaking after indecorum in debate. (Section 239, p. 257.)

(17) Filling of blanks. (Section 214, p. 228.)

(18) A request of any kind.

(19) Raising a question of privilege. (Section 221, p. 237; Section 223, p. 239.)

(20) Division of the assembly. (Section 150, p. 163.)

(21) Take up a question out of its order. (Section 112, p. 143.)

(22) Nominations. (Section 115-122, pp. 145-147.)

205. **Order of Amending.** When a resolution or proposition is pending, a primary amendment may be offered and then an amendment to that amendment may be offered. The first amendment is called a primary amendment and the amendment to that amendment is called a secondary amendment. When these two amendments are pending, no further amendment is in order. One who intends to offer an amendment when it is in order may rise and give notice of his intention to offer another amendment of a different nature by saying, "Mr. President, I give notice that at the proper time I intend to introduce an amendment which will have for its purpose (here state the purpose of the intended amendment)."

The natural order of amending a proposition is to begin at the beginning and amend each paragraph or division in order and then open the proposition to amendments as a whole. If there is a caption or a preamble, amendments are made to these last. When an amendment to the amendment has been adopted, the next question is on the adoption of the amendment as amended. When all amendments to the main motion have been adopted, the question is on the main motion as amended. While there can be but one primary and one secondary amendment pending at a time, as soon as these are disposed of, other primary and secondary amendments may be offered until the proposition is perfected or until debate is cut off.

206. Effect of Amendments That Fail to Be Adopted.
Those amendments offered to a certain part of a pending proposition that fail to be adopted do not preclude the offering of other amendments to the same part of the proposition. The amendment may be similar to the amendment lost but it must not be identical. For example: When a motion to strike out certain words and insert others in lieu thereof has failed, another amendment may be offered striking out the same words, but the words sought to be inserted must be different.

207. Propriety of Amendments. The subject matter which amendments may cover is wide. The general rule is that amendments must be germane to the proposition which they seek to amend, that is, have some direct bearing on the proposition. The chairman may hold an amendment out of order which does not relate directly to the pending proposition. No amendment is in order which would strike out or insert words which would destroy the sense of the proposition. No amendment is in order on a question which the organization has already considered and disposed of. No amendment is in order which would substitute one form of amendment for another form, or substitute one kind of motion for another.

208. Types of Amendments. The motion to amend of necessity takes many forms depending upon the proposition proposed to be amended and upon the kind of change the mover of the amendment wishes to make.

They are:

   (1) To add
   (2) To insert
   (3) To strike out
   (4) To strike out and insert in lieu thereof
   (5) To substitute
   (6) To fill a blank

209. Form of Amendments.

(1) To Add:

To amend by adding means the addition of new words or parts to the pending proposition.

"I move that the resolution be amended by adding the words 'as long as the season lasts' to the paragraph under consideration."

(2) To Insert:

To amend by inserting means the placing of new words within a sentence or a paragraph of the pending proposition.

"I move to amend the resolution by inserting the words 'and special' after the word 'regular' and before the word 'member.' "

(3) To Strike Out:

To amend by striking out means striking out certain words or parts from the pending proposition.

"I move to amend the resolution by striking out the word 'regular.' "

(4) To Strike Out and Insert in Lieu Thereof:

To amend by striking out certain words and inserting others in lieu thereof is the form of amendment used when the mover wishes to take out words or parts of the pending proposition and put in other words or parts in lieu of the words stricken out. This motion cannot be divided.

"I move to amend the resolution by striking out the word 'accommodate' and inserting in lieu thereof the words 'remain open to.'"

(5) To Substitute:

To amend by substituting an entire new paragraph or even an entire new resolution on the same subject is in order. The friends and proponents of the substituted part should take care to perfect the substitute by amendments before it is adopted, as a substitute can not be amended after it is voted on.*

"I move to amend the resolution by striking out the paragraph under consideration and substituting the following paragraph. (Here read the paragraph to be substituted.)"

(6) Filling Blanks.

Filling blanks is a method of amending by inserting. It differs from other forms of the motion to amend in that a member neither needs to secure recognition to send up a number to fill a blank nor does his number need to be seconded. This method of amending is used when a number is to be decided on, a date to be agreed to, an amount of money to be determined, or a name to be selected by the group.

---

*After an amendment is adopted and becomes a part of the main proposition, it cannot again be amended except by adding to it. The only way by which an assembly can change an amendment that has been adopted other than amending it by addition is to move a reconsideration of the vote by which the assembly adopted the amendment.

The motion to amend by filling blanks can be made in two different ways:

(1) The chair may on his own initiative say, "If there is no objection, this matter will be treated as the filling of a blank."

(2) In the event the chair does not take the initiative here, a member may seek recognition and say, "Mr. Chairman, I ask that the matter be treated as the filling of a blank, by general consent."

If general consent is not given to treating a matter as the filling of a blank, some member may make a motion that this procedure be used, saying, "Mr. President, I move that the figure in the resolution be treated as a blank."

If this motion is adopted, or if general consent authorizes treating the matter as a blank, the various members send up the figures they propose to fill the blank. They are put to a vote in the order determined by the chair. (See Section 214, p. 228.)

210. **To Insert and to Add.** When an amendment is to be offered inserting or adding certain words, the form of the amendment should be perfected before any vote is taken. After words have been inserted or added they may not be changed except by moving to strike out the entire paragraph or a sufficient portion to give the amendment a different meaning; or the motion may be combined with a motion to insert other words in place of the words struck out.

In other words, when certain words have been adopted as part of a resolution, another motion may not be made involving the same question, but a motion may be made to reconsider the vote by which these words were inserted.

If a motion to insert certain words fails of adoption, another motion may be made to insert these words and additional words, or to insert them in place of other words, but the new motion must embody a new proposition.

211. To Strike Out. The motion to amend by striking out can be applied only to consecutive words. If the words to be struck out are separated by words which should be retained in the proposition, the maker must either make several motions to amend by striking out or make a single motion to strike out and insert. By this latter motion the entire sentence or sentences containing all the words to be struck out will be removed and the words to be retained will be inserted again. (See Section 212, p. 227, To Strike Out and Insert in Lieu Thereof.)

The motion to amend by striking out may itself be amended by a motion to amend by striking out. If the amendment to the amendment is adopted, it will lessen the number of words to be struck out of the main proposition. Thus words contained in the amendment to the amendment will be retained in the main proposition if both motions are adopted. For example: A motion to amend by striking out the words "except the secretary and the parliamentarian" might be amended by striking out the words "except the secretary." If both amendments are adopted, the words "except the secretary" will remain in the main proposition and the words "and the parliamentarian" will be struck out.

If a motion to amend by striking out is adopted, the same words cannot be inserted later unless the proposition has been so changed meanwhile that it is a different proposition. If the motion to amend by striking out fails, other motions may be made striking out some of the same words but not all, and a motion may be made striking out the same words and inserting others.

212. To Strike Out and Insert in Lieu Thereof. A motion to amend by striking out and inserting in lieu thereof must be in the nature of a transfer. Either the same words must be struck out in one place and inserted in another or words struck out may be replaced by inserting different words in the same place. Either the words or the place must be the same.

The motion to amend by striking out and inserting may be made after a motion to strike out has failed or a motion to insert has failed, even though the words under consideration are the same. When a motion to amend by striking out and inserting fails, it may be followed by a simple motion to strike out the same words or a simple motion to insert the same words. Another motion to strike out and insert may be made after a motion to strike out and insert has failed provided that either the words to be inserted or the words to be struck out differ from those in the motion that failed.

The motion to amend by striking out and inserting may be amended. This is done by dividing the motion temporarily, allowing the motion to amend by striking out to be amended and then the motion to amend by inserting to be amended. The motion to amend by striking out and inserting must be put to the vote as a whole. If it is adopted, the words struck out may not again be inserted nor the words inserted later be struck out unless the proposition has been so changed as to be a different proposition.

213. **To Substitute.** The motion to amend by substituting is used when it is desired to strike out and insert a whole paragraph. It may be used also to substitute an entire proposition for the pending proposition. The procedure is the same whether the substitution is for a paragraph or for an entire resolution. When the motion to amend by substituting has been made and before a vote is taken, both the original paragraph and the substitute paragraph must be perfected. The original paragraph is open to amendments which are considered as secondary amendments. Then the substitute paragraph is open to amendments. After the substitute has been perfected, the question will be put on substitution, in this manner, "As many as favor amending the original motion by adopting the substitute will say 'aye'." After the chair completes the question and announces the vote, if the substitute has been adopted, the question will come next on the adoption of the motion as substituted. If the substitute fails, the original proposition is still before the assembly.

214. **Filling Blanks.** Filling blanks is a form of the motion to amend. The suggestions for filling the blank are not treated as amendments but as propositions independent one of the other. A motion to create a blank is not debatable. It cannot be amended, although a mem-

ber may move to fill the blank in some specified manner.
Each suggestion is in the nature of an amendment and
as such is debatable.

When a matter is to be determined, upon which there
are many opinions, this method permits all members to
offer their suggestions and gives the organization notice
of the various suggestions from which they will have an
opportunity to select. If the usual form of amendment
were used, it would not be possible for the group to recognize more than three separate propositions at a time—
that is, an original proposition, a motion to amend, and
a motion to amend the amendment.

The order in which the chair puts the question varies
according to circumstances; for example:

(1) When a date is to be agreed to, the members propose their suggestions and the secretary lists the suggestions chronologically. The chair puts the question first
on the date farthest distant and proceeds to put the question on each date until a majority have agreed to a date.

(2) When a number is to be determined, all numbers
are received and arranged numerically. The chair puts
the question on the greatest number first and continues
to put the question on each successively lower numeral
until a number is agreed to.

(3) When a name is to be selected, all names are sent
up. The secretary keeps the names in the order they
come to the desk. When all names are in, the chair puts
the question on the name received first and so on until
one name receives a majority.

(4) If several names are to be selected and more

names are suggested than are required, the chair puts
the vote on the names in the order they were received
at the desk until the necessary number of names has
been selected.

(5) When a sum of money is to be determined by
the filling of blanks, the presiding officer should consider the facts in the case and be guided thereby as to
whether he shall put the smallest amount or the largest
amount of money to the vote first.

215. Correction of the Minutes.

Minutes are usually
corrected informally, but if objection should be made it
is necessary to adopt a motion to correct them, which is,
in effect, an amendment. They may be corrected as many
times as the organization sees fit without regard to the
number of times they have been corrected or the time
that has elapsed since the minutes were approved by a
two-thirds vote or by a majority vote after prior notice
has been given. (See Section 236, p. 255.)

POSTPONE INDEFINITELY

216. Rank.

This motion is sixth and last in rank of the
subsidiary motions. It requires a second. The maker
must obtain recognition.

Purpose: To dispose of or defeat the main question
without waiting for the vote on adoption. It postpones
the proposition for the length of the session.

Effect: This motion, if adopted, defeats the main
proposition. A question that has been postponed indefinitely has the same status as a question that has
failed of adoption.

Form: "I move that the pending resolution (here state the nature of the resolution) be postponed indefinitely."

Yields: The motion yields to all privileged and incidental motions and to all the subsidiary motions.

Precedence: It takes precedence of nothing except the principal question which it seeks to postpone.

Debatable: This motion opens the merits of the main question to debate.

Motions Applicable: This motion cannot be amended nor can it have any other subsidiary motion applied to it except the motion for the previous question. The incidental question to extend or limit debate can also be made to apply to the motion to postpone indefinitely.

The adoption of the motion to commit while the motion to postpone indefinitely is pending eliminates the latter motion. If a motion to table is adopted when a motion to postpone indefinitely is pending the latter motion goes to the table with the proposition tabled. Likewise, if a motion to postpone to a certain time is adopted while the motion to postpone indefinitely is pending, the latter motion is postponed.

An affirmative vote on the motion to postpone indefinitely may be reconsidered, but a negative vote may not. Since this motion opens the merits of the main question to debate, it cannot be renewed.

Adoption: A majority vote is sufficient.

STUDY AND DISCUSSION TOPICS

1.   What is the nature and purpose of subsidiary motions?

2.   In what relation do they stand to main motions?

3.   Give an example of a main motion with four subsidiary motions pending and tell how you would dispose of them.

4.   Give an example of the motion for the previous question applying to a main motion and two subsidiary motions.

5.   How many forms may the motion to amend take? List them and give an illustration of each.

6.   What is the advantage in treating a proposition as a blank?

7.   How do blanks differ from other types of amendments?

8.   When several types of committees are proposed, in what order should the several proposals be considered?

9.   How may a motion to commit be amended? Illustrate the several methods.

10.   How may the adoption of the motion to postpone require a two-thirds vote when ordinarily it requires a majority vote for adoption?

11.   What propositions may be considered after the previous question has been ordered?

12.   Why is a motion to lay on the table considered a motion of a double purpose?

CHAPTER XII.

PRIVILEGED QUESTIONS

DEFINITION

217. Privileged questions are those questions which refer to the privileges laid down by parliamentary law for the conduct of the organization and questions of privilege which have to do with the rights and privileges of the members as a whole, and the privileges of an individual member.

FIX THE TIME TO WHICH TO ADJOURN

218. **When Privileged:** This motion is privileged if made when another question is pending or if made when no provision has been made for an adjourned meeting on the same or the next day. The conditions outlined below apply only to the motion when privileged.

Rank: First in rank of privileged motions, it may be made even after the motion to adjourn has been made and put to a vote if the result has not yet been announced. It requires a second. The maker must obtain recognition.

Purpose: To provide another meeting (usually called an adjourned meeting) which will be a continuation of the current meeting.

Effect: If adopted, it fixes another meeting time which must not be beyond the time already fixed for a regular meeting. It may also fix the place for the adjourned meeting.

Form: "I move that when we adjourn, we adjourn to nine o'clock a. m. tomorrow."

Yields: To nothing.

Precedence: Takes precedence of all other motions.

Debatable: Not debatable when privileged.

Motions Applicable: Can be amended only by changing the time to which to adjourn. No other subsidiary motion may be applied. Vote on the motion to fix the time to which to adjourn can be reconsidered.

Adoption: A majority vote is required for adoption.

ADJOURN

219. **When Privileged:** The motion to adjourn is always privileged with these two exceptions:

(1) When it is qualified in any way.

(2) When because of lack of provision for another meeting the motion to adjourn would dissolve the assembly as in a mass meeting.

When in Order: It is always in order except:

(1) When a member has the floor and refuses to yield for the motion to adjourn.

(2) When the assembly is voting (though it may be

made before the results of the vote have been announced).

(3) When no business has been transacted since a motion to adjourn was made.

Rank: Second in rank of the privileged motions. It requires a second. The maker must obtain recognition.

Purpose: To adjourn the meeting.

Effect: If adopted, the motion forces the chair to declare the meeting adjourned.

Form: "I move that the meeting stand adjourned." The chair may adjourn the assembly without a motion when the time previously fixed for adjournment arrives.

Yields: It yields only to the motion to fix the time to which to adjourn.

Precedence: Takes precedence of all motions except the motion to fix the time to which to adjourn.

Debatable: Undebatable when privileged.

Motions Applicable: Cannot be amended nor can it have any other subsidiary motion applied to it. The vote cannot be reconsidered. The motion can be renewed after progress has been made in consideration or in debate.

Adoption: A majority vote is sufficient for adoption. This is one of the three motions which may be adopted when no quorum is present. The others are a call of the house, and a motion to fix the time to which to adjourn.

TAKE A RECESS

220. When Privileged. If made when other business is before the assembly, it is privileged. The conditions outlined below apply only to the motion when privileged.*

Rank: This motion is third in rank of the privileged motions. It must be seconded. The maker of the motion must obtain recognition.

Purpose: Its purpose is to provide a recess or intermission in the proceedings.

Effect: If this motion is adopted, the chair declares that the assembly stands recessed until the time set as the end of the recess. When the chair calls the meeting to order at the end of a recess, business is taken up exactly as though no recess had been taken.

Form: "I move that the meeting stand recessed until two o'clock p.m. to-day."

Yields: To the motion to adjourn and the motion to fix the time to which to adjourn.

Precedence: Takes precedence of all other motions except the two privileged motions, (1) fix the time to which to adjourn, and (2) adjourn, to which it yields.

Debatable: No.

Motions Applicable: No subsidiary motion can be applied to the motion to take a recess except the motion to amend. It can be amended by changing the length of the recess. The vote cannot be reconsidered. The

---

*A motion to take a recess at some future time or a motion to take a recess made when no business is before the assembly is not privileged. It is an incidental main motion and is debatable. Other motions can apply to it as to any incidental main motion.

motion can be renewed after some progress has been made in debate or consideration.

Adoption: A majority vote is sufficient for adoption.

When a recess has been provided for in the program or order of business, the chair may declare a recess when the appointed time arrives without waiting for a motion. At that time the taking of a recess may be postponed, but a two-thirds vote is required. Failing to take the recess as set in the orders of the day is much the same as suspension of the rules and therefore requires the same vote.

QUESTIONS OF PRIVILEGE: GENERAL PRIVILEGE

221. **Rank.** A question of general privilege is one which relates to the rights of the members collectively. It is fourth in rank of the privileged questions.

A question of general privilege can be made without obtaining recognition. It does not require a second. If it concerns some action which should be considered at once, it may even interrupt a speaker.

When a question of privilege is stated, the chair determines whether it should interrupt pending business if made when another matter is before the assembly. His decision is subject to an appeal.

Purpose: A question of general privilege is raised to secure to the assembly some right or to correct some impropriety or some violation of its rights.

Effect: If the chair finds that it is a question of proper privilege, he allows it to interrupt pending business.

Form: A member rises to his feet and, without waiting for recognition, says: "Mr. Chairman, I rise to a question of general privilege."

The Chair: "State your question of general privilege."

The member states his question and the chair determines its propriety, subject to appeal.

Yields: To the motions to adjourn, to fix the time to which to adjourn, and to take a recess.

Precedence: Takes precedence of all motions except the motions to adjourn, to fix time to which to adjourn, and to take a recess.

Debatable: The raising of a question of privilege may not be debated. An appeal from the decision of the chair concerning a question of privilege is debatable. A main motion made as a result of the question of privilege is debatable without regard to the proposition which the question of privilege interrupted.

Motions Applicable: A motion made as a result of a question of privilege is open to amendment and to all other subsidiary motions as is any main motion. It can be disposed of by vote or by one of the subsidiary motions without affecting the proposition interrupted, which is resumed as soon as the question of privilege is disposed of. The vote can be reconsidered.

Adoption: A question of privilege is determined by the chair, subject to appeal, or a motion is made to correct the situation complained of. The raising of a question of privilege never comes to a vote but the motion made as a result of the question is voted on as a main motion. A majority vote is sufficient for its adoption.

222. Use of General Privilege in Question of "No Quorum."

The most commonly raised question of general privilege is the question of "no quorum." Whenever the absence of a quorum is discovered, the only action permissible is to adjourn or to put on a call of the house and send for the absent members. No vote may be taken after the absence of a quorum is discovered except on the motions for a call of the house, to adjourn, or to fix the time to which to adjourn.*

QUESTIONS OF PRIVILEGE: PERSONAL PRIVILEGE

223. **Rank.** A question of personal privilege yields to a question of general privilege. It can be made without obtaining recognition and does not require a second. Only one question of privilege may be pending at a time.

Purpose: To bring before the assembly some question as to the honor, reputation, safety, etc., of a member. The question must relate to the person as a member or to charges against him which affect him as a member.

Effect: If the chair finds it a question of proper privilege, he may adjust the difficulty, subject to appeal, or permit a motion to be made to correct the situation complained of.

Form: The member rises to his feet and, without

---

*See footnote, Sec. 109, p. 142.

waiting for recognition, says: "Mr. Chairman, I rise to a question of personal privilege," to which the chair replies, "State your question of privilege." The member states the question and the chair decides, subject to appeal, if the question of privilege is a proper one.

Yields: To the motions to adjourn, to fix the time to which to adjourn, to take a recess, and to a question of general privilege.

Precedence: Takes precedence of all motions except to adjourn, to fix the time to which to adjourn, to take a recess, and questions of general privilege.

Debatable: The raising of the question is not debatable; but the question when raised is debatable as is any main motion.

Motions Applicable: A main motion made as a result of the question of privilege may be disposed of by vote or by any of the subsidiary motions without having any effect on the main proposition which was interrupted. The vote can be reconsidered.

Adoption: A majority vote is sufficient for adoption of a motion made as a result of a question of privilege.

224. **Parliamentary Inquiry.** The most commonly used form of personal privilege is the parliamentary inquiry. A member in doubt on any point as to the procedure may rise and say, "Mr. Chairman, I rise to a parliamentary inquiry."

The chair replies, "State your inquiry."

The member states his inquiry and the reply of the chair is final. This question cannot interrupt one who has the floor. The parliamentary inquiry must be related to the pending proposition.

CALL FOR THE ORDERS OF THE DAY

225. **Definition.** Orders of the day are those propositions which are a part of the established order of business: the propositions set as special orders and the propositions set as general orders.

Special orders always come before general orders because a special order is set by a two-thirds vote and in effect suspends everything which interferes with its consideration. General orders are made by a majority vote. (Section 194, p. 209.)

A special order is considered at the time appointed for its consideration regardless of what is pending. If the chair does not announce the special order when the time set for its consideration arrives, any member may call for the orders of the day; or if the order of business is varied from in any way, a call for the orders of the day may be made.

226. **When In Order.** A call for the orders of the day is not in order unless there is a variation from the order of business. When only general orders are waiting, the call for orders of the day cannot interrupt a pending question, though it can be made after a motion has been made but before it has been stated by the chair.

When a special order has been set and the time arrives for its consideration, a call for the orders of the day can interrupt pending business or a speaker but cannot interrupt voting.

227. **Rank.** This motion is sixth in rank of the privi-

leged motions. It does not require a second. The maker
need not obtain recognition. It must not be qualified
in any way because a motion to take up a particular
part of the orders of the day, or to consider some certain question is not a privileged motion.

Purpose: To force the assembly to follow its own
rules concerning order of business.

Effect: If this motion is adopted, the assembly proceeds at once to the orders of the day. Orders of the
day refer to the established order of business.

Form: A member rises and without waiting for recognition says: "Mr. Chairman, I call for the orders of
the day."

The chair replies, "Shall the orders of the day be considered now?"

Yields: It yields to the motions to adjourn, to fix
time to which to adjourn, and to take a recess. It yields
also to questions of privilege, and to a motion to reconsider, or to the calling up of a motion to reconsider
made previously.

Precedence: Takes precedence of all motions except
those mentioned above, to which it yields.

Debatable: No.

Motions Applicable: No subsidiary motions are applicable. Affirmative vote cannot be reconsidered.

Adoption: The question is put: "Will the assembly
proceed to the orders of the day?" If two-thirds or more
vote "no," the orders of the day may be disregarded. If
more than one-third of those voting say "aye," the as-

sembly must obey its own rules and proceed to the orders of the day.

STUDY AND DISCUSSION TOPICS

1. What is the difference between privileged questions and questions of privilege? Illustrate.

2. Can you think of any reasons for considering the motions to fix the time to which to adjourn, adjourn, and to recess as privileged questions? State one reason for each.

3. Name the privileged questions and give the object of each.

4. Name the two questions of privilege. Which takes precedence of the other?

5. Give an example of a question of general privilege, a question of personal privilege.

6. Is there any reason for allowing one to take precedence of the other?

7. Explain the call for the orders of the day. What is meant by orders of the day, and when may they be called for?

8. How does the chair state the question on call for the orders of the day?

9. What vote is required to maintain the orders of the day? Why?

10. Name three matters that would be termed questions of general privilege. Name three that would be termed questions of personal privilege.

CHAPTER XIII.

INCIDENTAL MOTIONS

QUESTIONS OF ORDER

228. **Rank.** Questions of order are incidental motions. They may be made when some one else has the floor, even interrupting a speech or a report. No second is required. The maker need not obtain recognition.

Purpose: To call to the attention of the chair a departure from orderly proceeding on the part of the chair or another member.

Effect: It places responsibility on the chair, whose duty it is to see that rules of order are enforced, to decide whether or not the question raised is a proper one.

Form: A member stands and says: "Mr. Chairman, I rise to a point of order." (He then takes his seat.)

The chair replies, "State your point of order." The member stands and states his point of order and then sits down to hear the ruling of the chair.

Yields: To privileged motions and the motion to lay on the table.

Precedence: It takes precedence of the pending question out of which it arises.

Debatable: A question of order is decided by the chair without debate though he may ask advice of a member who should give the advice sitting to avoid the appearance of debate.

If the chair submits a question of order to the assembly for decision, the question of order is open to debate if an appeal from the decision of the chair on that point would have been debatable. Therefore it is debatable except when it relates to indecorum, priority of business, or transgression of the rules of speaking, or when it is made during a division of the assembly, or when an undebatable question is immediately pending. (See Appeal, Section 229, p. 246.)

Motions Applicable: If the question is submitted to the assembly and is debatable the previous question may be applied. The vote on a question of order may be reconsidered. The motion to lay on the table may be made while a question of order is pending. It applies to the main question and if adopted carries the question of order to the table with the main question.

Adoption: Questions of order are decided by the chair, no vote being necessary unless the question is given to the assembly. A majority vote is then sufficient.

APPEAL

229. **Rank.** An appeal must be made immediately after the ruling which it seeks to repeal. The person making the appeal need not have recognition. An appeal may be made from any decision of the chair except when another appeal is pending. In that event, a question of order may be raised but it must be decided by the chair without debate. The correctness of the ruling on the question of order may be brought up later when no other business is pending.

An appeal must be seconded.*

Purpose: To reverse a decision of the chair.

Effect: The question on appeal is stated.** "Shall the decision of the chair stand as the judgment of the assembly?" If the majority vote is negative, the decision of the chair is reversed.

---

*In large organizations, it is necessary to require that an appeal be seconded by several persons as appeals could be used to delay the business of the organization if two persons could appeal. Each organization should provide in its by-laws or rules of order for a certain number of members to second an appeal. The number of members required to second an appeal should be determined by the size of the active membership.

**The presiding officer may call some member to the chair to put the question but he is not obliged to do so.

Form: "Mr. Chairman, I appeal from the decision of the chair."

Yields: It yields to privileged motions and to the motion to lay on the table. It yields also to the raising of a question of order which must then be decided by the chair without debate.

Precedence: It takes precedence of all main motions and all subsidiary motions except the motion to lay on the table, and all other incidental motions except the raising of a question of order.

Debatable: Yes; except: (1) When the question from which appeal is taken is not debatable. (2) When previous question has been moved. (3) When it relates to indecorum, transgression of the rules of speaking, or the priority of business. (4) When a vote is being taken by division of the house.

The chair may state his reasons for the decision, whether the appeal is debatable or not. When debatable no one may speak more than once.

Motions Applicable: An appeal cannot be amended. The vote on an appeal may be reconsidered.

When an appeal is debatable the previous question may be moved on the appeal. An appeal may be laid on the table. If the main proposition would be affected by a reversal of the ruling being appealed, the main proposition goes to the table with the appeal. On the other hand when the main proposition would not be affected by the decision on the appeal, the appeal may go to the table alone which has the effect of sustaining the judgment of the chair as long as the appeal remains tabled.

Adoption: The question is put: "As many as favor sustaining the judgment of the chair will say 'aye.' (The votes are counted.) Those opposed will say 'no.' " (The votes are counted.) If there is a tie vote the chair is sustained, or the chair may vote to make a tie. The decision of the chair stands unless reversed by the majority, the chair being permitted to vote.

OBJECTION TO THE CONSIDERATION OF A QUESTION

230. **Rank.** Objection to the consideration of a question must be made immediately and before the assembly has debated the question. The maker need not obtain recognition. It does not require a second.

Purpose: To prevent the consideration of some proposition in which the assembly has no interest or which the members think would be unwise to consider. It applies only to a main motion which may be an order of the day, never to incidental main motions.

Effect: To remove the proposition from the consideration of the assembly at that session.

Form: Immediately after the main motion is made the member wishing to object rises and says: "Mr. Chairman, I object to the consideration of this question."

Yields: To privileged motions and to the motion to lay on the table.*

---

*When an objection to the consideration of a main motion is made, and a motion to table is made, the motion to table applies to the main motion and, if carried, the objection to the consideration of the question goes with the main proposition to the table. When taken from the table, the question of consideration is the immediately pending question and yields to nothing but privileged motions.

Precedence: Takes precedence of all questions except questions of order, appeals, privileged motions, and the motion to lay on table.

Debatable: No.

Motions Applicable: No subsidiary motion may be applied. Negative but not affirmative vote may be reconsidered.

Adoption: The question is put: "Will the assembly consider the proposition? Those in favor of considering the proposition will say 'aye.' (The vote is taken.) Those opposed to considering the proposition will say 'no.'"

If the vote is two-thirds negative, the whole matter is dismissed for the session.

THE READING OF PAPERS

231. Rank. A member must get the permission of the assembly to have miscellaneous papers read to the assembly for their enlightenment. This permission may be given by general consent; but if anyone objects, a motion to secure permission to read the papers may be made. The maker must obtain recognition. The motion requires a second.

Purpose: To secure permission of the assembly to have papers read.

Effect: Gives consent, if adopted, to have the papers read.

Form: "I move that the clerk read the papers relating to—(here state the nature of the papers)."

Yields: To privileged motions.

Precedence: Takes precedence of the question out of which it arose. If it is an incidental main motion, that is, an independent motion, it is in order at any time new business is in order.

Debatable: No.

Motions Applicable: It cannot be amended nor can it have any other subsidiary motion applied to it.

Adoption: A majority vote is sufficient for adoption.

WITHDRAWAL OF A MOTION

232. **Rank.** This is an incidental motion. It does not require a second. The maker must obtain recognition.

Purpose: After a motion has been stated by the chair, it is before the assembly for consideration. If the maker wishes to withdraw it, modify it, or substitute another in its place, he may do so by general consent before any decision is reached on the motion. However, if anyone objects, general consent fails, and it is necessary to get the permission of the assembly to withdraw the motion or to change it in any way.

Effect: When a motion is withdrawn it is the same as though it had never been made, and it may be presented again as a new motion. The minutes need not record the making of the motion and its subsequent withdrawal.

Form: "I move that the assembly give its permission for the withdrawal of this motion."

Yields: To privileged motions.

Precedence: It takes precedence of other incidental

motions and of subsidiary motions. Motions pending to a motion withdrawn are automatically withdrawn.

Debatable: No.

Motions Applicable: This motion cannot be amended nor have any other subsidiary motion applied to it. An affirmative vote on withdrawal of a motion cannot be reconsidered.

Adoption: Permission to withdraw a motion is given by a majority vote.

SUSPENSION OF THE RULES

233. **Rank.** This is an incidental motion. It may be made at any time when no question is pending or when the question to which it is incidental is pending. The rules established in the constitution and by-laws and in the fundamental principles of parliamentary law can never be suspended. However, some constitutions and by-laws provide for the suspension of certain rules. The maker must obtain recognition. The motion requires a second.

Purpose: To suspend rules which interfere with some definite action which the assembly is contemplating. The motion to suspend the rules should state the purpose for which the suspension is asked.

Effect: If adopted, this motion suspends the rules which would interfere with the action under consideration. The rules are suspended for this one action alone.

Form: "I move to suspend the rules that interfere with—(here state the nature of the proposition)."

Yields: To all the privileged motions except calls

for the orders of the day. It also yields to the motion to lay on the table and to motions incidental to itself.

Precedence: It takes precedence of the question which the rule to be suspended interfered with.

Debatable: No.

Motions Applicable: None of the subsidiary motions can be applied to it. A motion to reconsider a vote on the suspension of a rule is never in order. It is not in order to move the suspension of the rules on the same proposition twice in one meeting. Objection to consideration may not be made. The motion to suspend the rules on the proposition can be renewed at an adjourned meeting even though the adjourned meeting takes place on the same calendar day.

Adoption: A two-thirds vote is required for adoption. A rule, the suspension of which would give a right to any group as small as one-third, should require unanimous consent for suspension.

TO LIMIT OR CLOSE DEBATE

234. Rank.   This is an incidental motion.* It may

---

*Robert's Rules of Order Revised makes the motions to limit or extend the limits of debate subsidiary ones. Subsidiary motions are motions that apply to other motions. The motions to limit or extend the limits of debate regulate procedure rather than dispose of motions. The motion for the previous question is a subsidiary motion because it applies to a motion or series of motions. The motion to limit debate limits the amount of time to be spent in discussion of a motion or of a series of motions. Inasmuch as subsidiary motions are defined as motions made for the purpose of disposing of other motions, and incidental motions are defined as motions which arise out of other business, this text takes the position that the motions to limit or extend the limits of debate are incidental.

In other words, the motion to limit or close debate applies to debate in general, while the motion for the previous question which closes debate applies to a named question or series of questions. In Congress, the motions to limit or close debate are used to regulate the calendar.

be made only when the immediately pending question is debatable. It applies to all incidental motions, all subsidiary motions and the motion to reconsider, even though the motion to reconsider is made after the motion to limit debate. The maker of the motion must obtain recognition. The motion requires a second.

When a motion closing debate at a certain hour or limiting debate to a certain time is adopted, the motions to postpone and to commit cannot be moved until the motions affecting debate have been reconsidered.

Purpose: To limit the number of speeches or the length of the speeches, or set an hour at which debate shall be closed.

Effect: Debate is limited or closed in the way specified in the motion. The chair must put the question at the time set. After the motion to limit or close debate has been adopted, the motions to commit and to postpone the main question cannot be made unless the vote to limit the debate has been reconsidered.

Form: "I move that debate on this question be closed at four o'clock p. m. to-day."

Yields: To privileged motions and motions incidental to itself and to the motions to lay on the table and the previous question.

Precedence: Takes precedence of the question which it seeks to affect.

Debatable: No.

Motions Applicable: It may be amended but can have no other subsidiary motion applied. A motion to extend the limit of debate may be applied to this motion as an amendment if there is no conflict. After it has been adopted, the motion to extend the limit may be made if there is no conflict. The motion to limit debate may be reconsidered even after debate has taken place under the limitation. If the motion to reconsider is lost, it may be made again after progress in debate.

Adoption: A two-thirds vote is required as it is practically a suspension of the rules of free debate.

TO EXTEND THE LIMIT OF DEBATE

235. **Rank.** This is an incidental motion.* It may be made only when the immediately pending question is debatable and applies only to the pending question unless others are specified. The maker of the motion must obtain recognition. The motion requires a second.

Purpose: To extend the limit of debate, that had been set previously.

Effect: If this motion is adopted, the limitation on debate is extended on the pending question or questions as specified in the motion.

Form: "I move that debate be extended until five o'clock p. m."

Yields: To privileged motions and motions incidental to itself; to the motions to lay on the table and the previous question.

---

*See Section 234, p. 252.

Precedence: Takes precedence of the question which it seeks to affect.

Debatable: No.

Motions Applicable: It may be amended but can have no other subsidiary motion applied. A motion to limit debate may be applied to this motion as an amendment if there is no conflict. The motion to extend the limit of debate may be reconsidered even after debate has taken place under the extended period. If the motion to reconsider is lost, it may be made again after progress in debate.

Adoption: A two-thirds vote is required as it is practically a suspension of the rules already setting a limit to debate.

APPROVAL OF THE RECORD OR CORRECTION OF THE MINUTES

236. The motion to correct the minutes or the record is in order after the minutes have been read or the record has been considered. Minutes are usually corrected at the instigation of the chair, who says, after a correction has been suggested, "If there is no objection the minutes will be corrected in this respect." If there is objection, a motion must be made that the minutes be corrected. A majority vote is sufficient to adopt a correction to the minutes.

The minutes may be corrected without regard to the time that has passed since the minutes were read and approved. If the time to reconsider the vote by which the minutes were approved or adopted has passed, it is necessary to adopt a further correction by a two-thirds vote or to notify all members that the correction will be suggested at the meeting. If previous notice has been given, only a majority vote is required for the adoption of the proposed correction to the minutes.

TO FIX METHOD OF VOTING WHEN A PROPOSITION IS PENDING

237. **Rank.** If made when a proposition or election is pending, this motion is incidental to the proposition or election and must be disposed of first. The maker must obtain recognition. The motion requires a second. It is in order even after nominations have been made.

Purpose: To decide upon the method of voting to be used in the pending election or proposition.

Effect: If adopted, this motion forces the assembly to vote by the method specified.

Form: "I move that the vote on this proposition be by ballot."

Yields: It yields to privileged motions.

Precedence: It takes precedence of the election or proposition out of which it arose.

Debatable: No.

Motions Applicable: It can be amended. No other subsidiary motion can be applied. The vote may not be reconsidered if any action has been taken as a result of the motion sought to be reconsidered.

Adoption: A majority vote is sufficient for adoption.

FIX METHOD OF MAKING NOMINATIONS WHEN AN ELECTION IS PENDING

238. **Rank.** When an election is pending this mo-

tion is incidental to the election. A second is required. The maker must obtain recognition.

Purpose: To fix method to be used in making nominations in the pending election.

Effect: Fixes the method specified as the one to be used in that election.

Form: "I move that nominations for the office of secretary be made by ballot."

Yields: To privileged motions.

Precedence: Takes precedence of the pending election.

Debatable: No.

Motions Applicable: No subsidiary motions except the motion to amend may be applied.

Adoption: A majority vote is sufficient for adoption.

CONTINUE SPEAKING AFTER INDECORUM

239. When a member has been found guilty of indecorum, the assembly must adopt a motion to give him leave to continue his remarks before the chair can recognize him for that purpose.

Rank: This motion has no particular rank. It is incidental to the continued debate of the member at fault and must be acted upon as soon as made. The motion to give a member permission to continue his remarks must be made immediately after the decision.

Purpose: To give the member permission to continue his remarks.

Effect: It allows a member interrupted by a question of order to proceed if the assembly so wills.

Form: "I move that the member be given permission to continue his remarks."

Yields: To privileged motions.

Precedence: It takes precedence of main motions.

Debatable: No.

Motions Applicable: No subsidiary motion may be applied.

Adoption: A majority vote is sufficient for adoption.

MOTION TO CLOSE NOMINATIONS

240. The motion to close nominations is incidental when nominations are being made. The member must secure recognition. The motion requires a second.

Purpose: To close the list of nominees.

Effect: Prevents the making of additional nominations.

Form: "I move that nominations for the office of president be closed."

Yields: To privileged motions.

Precedence: It takes precedence of a vote on the election of the nominees.

Debatable: No.

Motions Applicable: The motion to close nominations can be amended as to time but can have no other subsidiary motions applied to it. Since the motion can be renewed, a negative vote may not be reconsidered. The affirmative vote is never reconsidered because a motion to reopen nominations would have the same effect.

Adoption: It requires a two-thirds vote for adoption.

SPECIAL ORDER AS AN INCIDENTAL MOTION

241. **Rank.** When the proposition sought to be set as a special order is the immediately pending proposition, the motion to set as a special order is an incidental motion. The member must secure recognition. The motion requires a second.

Purpose: To postpone consideration of the measure until some future time, but insure its consideration by making it a special order.

Effect: If the motion to set as a special order is adopted, the proposition is placed on the calendar of the day and hour to which it was appointed.

Form: "I move that the pending proposition be set as a special order for three o'clock Thursday."

Yields: To privileged motions.

Precedence: It takes precedence of the vote on adoption of the question.

Debatable: No (See Debatable under Section 195, p. 213.)

Motions Applicable: The motion to amend can be applied to the motion to set as a special order. No other subsidiary motions can be applied. An affirmative vote can be reconsidered, but a negative one cannot.

Adoption: This motion requires a two-thirds vote for adoption, as it suspends the regular order of business.

DIVISION OF A QUESTION

242. **Rank.** This is an incidental motion. It can apply only to main motions and amendments. It can be made at any time when the question to be divided or the motion to postpone indefinitely is the immediately pending question. It can be made after the motion for the previous question has been ordered, although it is preferable to divide the question when it is first introduced or before any debate has taken place or other motions offered. When divided, each part is considered and voted on separately as though it had been offered alone. The formality of moving and voting on the motion to divide the question is rarely observed. The chair may divide a motion on his own initiative or a member may ask for general consent to divide a motion. If a motion to divide the question becomes necessary for the reasons that the chair did not divide the question on his own initiative, or general consent was refused, the motion to divide the question should specify how the question is to be divided. Another member may propose a different division. If several different divisions of the question are proposed, the matter should be treated as the filling of blanks. If the different proposals suggest different divisions, they are voted on in the order of their making. If they propose different numbers of questions, the proposal suggesting the greatest number of questions is voted on first. If a proposition contains several propositions but is so written that it cannot be divided without rewriting the resolution or proposition, it is not a divisible question.

Purpose: To permit the assembly to signify their

approval or disapproval of the various parts of the proposition.

Effect: If adopted, the several parts are considered and voted on as if they were introduced alone.

Form: "Mr. President, I move that the proposition be divided into three questions (here state the place of division)."

Yields: To all privileged, incidental and subsidiary motions except the motion to amend and the motion to postpone indefinitely.

Precedence: Takes precedence of the motion to postpone indefinitely.

Debatable: No.

Motions Applicable: The motion to amend is the only subsidiary motion which can be applied to it.

Adoption: A majority vote is required.

STUDY AND DISCUSSION TOPICS

1. Why are these motions called incidental motions?

2. What is the relation between incidental and incidental main motions?

3. Of what motions do incidental motions take precedence?

4. Why are the motions to limit, to extend, or to close debate incidental motions?

5. How does the making of the motion to appeal differ from other motions?

6. May the chair state his reasons for his decision on an appeal?

7. Objection to consideration may be applied to what class of motions? How is the question stated?

8. When is it necessary to have the assembly vote to hear papers read?

9. If a motion is withdrawn, is it in order to make the same motion again?

10. May a motion for suspension of the rules be applied to a provision in the constitution?

11. What vote is required to limit or extend the limit of debate?

12. How long after reading of the minutes may they be corrected?

13. Compare incidental and subsidiary motions as to purpose, effect, and motions applicable.

A GLOSSARY

By-laws. Rules covering procedure or business in a club or other organization.

Committee of the whole. The whole organization sitting in the form of a committee.

Constitution. Rules covering organization of a club or other organization.

Credentials. Papers showing the authority of an individual to act for a group or organization.

Debate. The discussion of a subject which has been introduced in the assembly.

Delegate (noun). One sent by a group to act for it.

Delegate (verb). To send some one to represent a group.

Ex officio. A person serving on a board, committee, or in an office because of a certain office which he holds.

Motions. Propositions introduced by members of an assembly calling for certain action to be taken.

Organic law. The fundamental laws of a nation, state or other organization.

Organization. A group of persons united for a common purpose.

Parliament. The law-making body of England corresponding to our Congress.

Parliamentary law. Laws by which the procedure of assemblies is regulated.

Petition. A written request addressed to an official or to an organization.

Precedence. Order of the rank of motions.

Proxy voting. Permission given by a member to another to vote in that member's place.

Quorum. The number of persons of a body which must be present in order to transact business legally.

Sessions. A session is a meeting or a group of adjourned or recessed meetings which ends without day (*sine die*).

Sine die. A Latin phrase meaning "without day." Adjourning *sine die* is adjourning without having set a day for a future meeting.

Viva voce vote. This means voting by voice, by saying "aye" or "no."

MOTIONS	Objection to Consideration	Must Have Recognition	Requires a Second
ADJOURN (When privileged. Section 219, p. 234.)	NO	YES	YES
ADJOURN (When not privileged. Sections 174-5, pp. 180-1.)	NO	YES	YES
ADJOURN, FIX TIME TO WHICH TO (When privileged. Section 218, p. 233.)	NO	YES	YES
ADJOURN, FIX TIME TO WHICH TO (When not privileged. Section 176, p. 181.)	NO	YES	YES
AMEND (Section 202, p. 218.)	NO	YES 2	YES 3
APPEAL (When debatable. Section 229, p. 246.)	NO	NO	YES 9
APPEAL (When undebatable. Section 229, p. 246.)	NO	NO	YES 9
CALL FOR THE ORDERS OF THE DAY (Section 225, p. 241.)	NO	NO	NO
COMMIT, REFER, OR RECOMMIT (Section 196, p. 214.)	NO	YES	YES
CONSTITUTION, BY-LAWS, RULES OF ORDER, to adopt	YES	YES	YES
CONSTITUTION, BY-LAWS, RULES OF ORDER, to amend (Section 180, p. 191.)	NO	YES	YES
CONTINUE SPEAKING AFTER INDECORUM IN DEBATE, leave to (Section 239, p. 257.)	NO	YES	YES
DEBATE, TO CLOSE, TO LIMIT, OR TO EXTEND LIMITS OF (Sections 234-235, pp. 252-4.)	NO	YES	YES
DIVISION OF THE QUESTION (Section 242, p. 260.)	NO	YES	YES
LAY ON THE TABLE (Section 186, p. 200.)	NO	YES	YES
MAIN MOTION (Section 171, p. 177.)	YES	YES	YES
MINUTES, TO APPROVE and TO CORRECT (Section 236, p. 255.)	NO	YES	YES
NOMINATIONS, TO CLOSE (Section 240, p. 258.)	NO	YES	YES
NOMINATIONS, FIX METHOD OF MAKING (When an election is pending. Section 238, p. 256.)	NO	YES	YES
NOMINATIONS, FIX METHOD OF MAKING (When no election is pending. Section 172, p. 178.)	NO	YES	YES
NOMINATIONS, TO OPEN (Section 115, p. 145) and TO REOPEN (Section 119, p. 146.)	NO	YES	YES
OBJECTION TO THE CONSIDERATION OF A QUESTION (Section 230, p. 248.)	NO	NO	NO

Debatable	Lay on Table	Previous Question	Postpone to a Certain Time	Commit, Refer or Recommit	Amend	Postpone Indefinitely	Reconsider	Requires Two-thirds Vote
NO	NO	NO	NO	NO	NO	NO	NO	NO
YES	YES	YES	YES	YES	YES	YES	NO	NO
NO	NO	NO	NO	NO	YES	NO	YES	NO
YES	YES	YES	YES	YES	YES	YES	YES 1	NO
YES 4	NO 5	YES 4	NO 6	NO 7	YES 8	NO	YES p. 188-91	NO
YES	YES 10	YES	YES 11	NO	NO	NO	YES	NO
NO	YES 10	NO	YES 11	NO	NO	NO	YES	NO
NO	NO	NO	NO	NO	NO	NO	12	13
YES 14	NO 15	YES	NO 16	NO	YES 17	NO	YES 18	NO
YES	YES	YES	YES	YES	YES	YES	19	NO
YES	YES	YES	YES	YES	YES 20	YES	19	YES 21
NO	NO	NO	NO	NO	NO	NO	YES	NO
NO	NO	NO	NO	NO	YES	NO	YES	YES
NO	NO	NO	NO	NO	YES	NO	NO	NO
NO	NO	NO	NO	NO	NO	NO	NO	NO
YES	YES	YES	YES	YES	YES	YES	YES	NO
YES	YES 22	YES	YES	NO	YES	YES	YES	NO 23
NO	NO	NO	NO	NO	YES	NO	NO 24	YES
NO	NO	NO	NO	NO	YES	NO	YES 25	NO
YES	YES	YES	YES	YES	YES	YES	YES 25	NO
NO	NO	NO	NO	NO	YES	NO	26	NO
NO	NO 27	NO	NO	NO	NO	NO	28	29

MOTIONS	Objection to Consideration	Must Have Recognition	Requires a Second
POSTPONE TO A CERTAIN TIME (Section 194, p. 209.)	NO	YES	YES
POSTPONE INDEFINITELY (Section 216, p. 230.)	NO	YES	YES
PREVIOUS QUESTION (Section 187, p. 203.)	NO	YES	YES
QUESTIONS OF ORDER (Section 228, p. 244.)	NO	NO	NO
QUESTIONS OF PRIVILEGE, GENERAL and PERSONAL (Sections 221 and 223, pp. 237 and 239.)	NO	NO	NO
RATIFY (Section 185, p. 196.)	NO	YES	YES
READING OF PAPERS, to permit (Section 231, p. 249.)	NO	YES	YES
RECONSIDER a debatable proposition (Section 179, p. 184.)	NO	YES	YES
RECONSIDER an undebatable proposition (Section 179, p. 184.)	NO	YES	YES
RESCIND (Section 177, p. 182.)	NO	YES	YES
SPECIAL ORDER, to make a (As an amendment to the motion to postpone and as an incidental motion. Sections 195 and 241, pp. 212 and 259.)	NO	YES	YES
SPECIAL ORDER, to make a (As an incidental main motion. Section 184, p. 195.)	NO	YES	YES
STANDING RULES, to adopt.	YES	YES	YES
STANDING RULES, to amend	NO	YES	YES
SUSPEND THE RULES (Section 233, p. 251.)	NO	YES	YES
TAKE A RECESS (When privileged, Section 220, p. 236.)	NO	YES	YES
TAKE A RECESS (When not privileged, Footnote, p. 236.)	NO	YES	YES
TAKE FROM THE TABLE (Section 181, p. 192.)	NO	YES	YES
VOTING, to FIX METHOD OF, when proposition is pending (Section 237, p. 256.)	NO	YES	YES
VOTING, to FIX METHOD OF, when no other proposition is pending (Section 173, p. 179.)	NO	YES	YES
WITHDRAW A MOTION, leave to (Section 232, p. 250.)	NO	YES	NO

Debatable	Lay on Table	Previous Question	Postpone to a Certain Time	Commit, Refer or Re-commit	Amend	Postpone Indefinitely	Reconsider	Requires Two-thirds Vote
YES 30	NO 31	YES	NO	NO	YES 32	NO	YES 33	NO 34
YES	NO 35	YES	NO 36	NO 37	NO	NO	38	NO
NO	NO 39	NO	NO	NO	NO Sec. 188	NO	YES 40	YES
NO 41	NO 42	43	NO	NO	NO	NO	YES 44	NO
YES	YES	YES	YES	YES	YES	YES	YES	NO
YES	YES	YES	YES	YES	YES 45	YES	YES	NO 46
NO	NO	NO	NO	NO	NO	NO	YES	NO
YES	YES 47	YES	YES 48	NO	NO	NO	49	NO
NO	YES 47	NO	YES 48	NO	NO	NO	49	NO
YES	YES	YES	YES	YES	YES	YES	50	51
NO	NO 52	NO	NO	NO	YES	NO	YES 53	54
YES	YES	YES	YES	YES	YES	YES	YES 53	YES
YES	YES	.YES	YES	YES	YES	YES	YES	NO
YES	YES	YES	YES	YES	YES	YES	YES	55
NO	NO	NO	NO	NO	NO	NO	NO	YES
NO	NO	NO	NO 56	NO	YES	NO	NO	NO
YES	YES	YES	YES 56	YES	YES	YES	NO	NO
NO	NO	NO	NO	NO	NO	NO	NO	NO
NO	NO	NO	NO	NO	YES	NO	YES 25	NO
YES	YES	YES	YES	YES	YES	YES	YES 25	NO
NO	NO	NO	NO	NO	NO	NO	57	NO

NOTES AND EXCEPTIONS TO THE "CHART OF MOTIONS"

Fix the Time to Which to Adjourn

1. A negative vote to fix the time to which to adjourn cannot be reconsidered because the motion can be renewed. However, an affirmative vote on the motion can be reconsidered.

Motion to Amend

2. Persons offering amendments must always have recognition except when the amendment takes the form of filling blanks.

3. A motion to amend by filling blanks does not require a second.

4. Amendments are debatable unless they are amendments to undebatable questions. When they are debatable, the previous question may apply.

5. The motion to lay on the table cannot be applied to the motion to amend; the motion to lay on the table may be made while the motion to amend is pending, and if the motion to lay on the table is adopted, the pending amendments go to the table with the main proposition.

6. When a motion to amend is pending and a motion is made to postpone to a certain time, the motion to postpone applies to the main question, and if it is adopted the pending amendment goes with the main question.

7. A motion to commit the main proposition may be made while an amendment is pending, and if the motion to commit carries, the amendment goes with the main proposition to the committee. An amendment cannot be committed alone.

8. An amendment to an amendment is in order, but the amendment to the amendment cannot be amended. Neither can amending by filling blanks be amended.

Appeal

9. Some organizations require more than one second for an appeal. (See footnote Sec. 229, p. 246.)

10. See "Motions Applicable" (Section 229, p. 247.)

11. When an appeal is pending and the motion to postpone to a certain time is made, it applies to the appeal. If the consideration of the main motion would be affected by the reversal of the ruling being appealed, the appeal cannot be postponed to a certain time without postponing the main proposition also.

Call for the Orders of the Day

12. Affirmative vote on motion to proceed to the orders of the day may not be reconsidered.

13. The question is put, "Will the assembly proceed to the orders of the day?" If the assembly does not wish to proceed to the orders of the day, it may decline to do so by a two-thirds negative vote.

Commit, Refer, or Recommit

14. Debate is limited to the propriety of commitment.

15. A motion to lay on the table may be made while the motion to commit is pending. If the motion to table carries, the motion to commit goes with the main proposition.

16. The motion to postpone to a certain time may be made while the motion to commit is pending, and if the main proposition is postponed, the motion to commit is postponed with it.

17. See Section 198, p. 216.

18. See Section 199, p. 217.

Adopt and Amend the Constitution

19. An affirmative vote on the adoption or on an amendment to the constitution, by-laws, or rules of order cannot be reconsidered.

20. An amendment to a pending amendment to the constitution, by-laws, or rules of order may be adopted without previous notice, provided it does not increase the proposed modification. (See footnote Sec. 23, p. 94.)

21. Either previous notice and two-thirds vote or a majority of the entire membership is usually required for adoption of an amendment.

Correction to the Minutes

22. Correction to the minutes may be laid on the table without taking the minutes with it.

23. If correction is made in the minutes after time has passed for a reconsideration of the vote on the minutes, it is necessary to make the correction by a two-thirds vote or a majority vote when previous notice of the correction has been given.

Motion to Close Nominations

24.   Since the motion can be renewed, a negative vote may not be reconsidered. The affirmative vote is never reconsidered because a motion to reopen nominations would have the same effect.

Motions to Fix Method of Voting and of Nominations

25.   The vote may not be reconsidered if any action has been taken as a result of the motion sought to be reconsidered.

Reopen Nominations

26.   An affirmative vote on this motion is not reconsidered because the motion to close nominations may be made. A negative vote can be reconsidered.

Objection to the Consideration of a Question

27.   When a main motion is introduced and an objection to the consideration of the question is made, the motion to lay on the table may be made. It applies to the main question and if the motion to lay on the table carries, the objection to the consideration of the question goes to the table with the main proposition.

28.   An affirmative vote on a motion to object to the consideration of a question may not be reconsidered. A negative vote may be reconsidered. In other words, if the objection is adopted, the assembly may reconsider.

29.   A two-thirds negative vote is necessary to object to the consideration of the question. Any vote less than two-thirds negative on the question, "Will the assembly consider the proposition?" permits the assembly to consider the question.

Postpone to a Certain Time

30.   The motion to postpone to a certain time permits of limited debate. The debate is limited to the propriety of the postponement.

31.   If a motion to table the main proposition is made while a motion to postpone to a certain time is pending, the motion to lay on the table is acted upon before the motion to postpone to a certain time; and if it carries, the motion to postpone goes with the main proposition.

32.   The motion can be amended as to the time, or amended by making it a special order.

33.   A matter postponed may be postponed again when the time arrives for its consideration, without reconsidering the previous vote.

34.   If a motion to postpone to a certain time is amended so that the proposition is made a special order, it requires a two-thirds vote.

Postpone Indefinitely

35. The motion to lay on the table may be made while the motion to postpone indefinitely is pending, and if carried, takes the motion to postpone indefinitely to the table with the main motion.

36. If the motion to postpone indefinitely is pending when a motion to postpone to a certain time is made and carried, the motion to postpone to a certain time carries the motion to postpone indefinitely with the main proposition.

37. If a motion to commit is made and carried while a motion to postpone indefinitely is pending, the motion to postpone indefinitely is ignored.

38. A negative vote on the motion to postpone indefinitely cannot be reconsidered.

Previous Question

39. The motion to lay on the table cannot apply to the motion for the previous question; however, when the previous question has been made and adopted on a series of motions, the motion to table may be made applying to the motions that have not been voted on under the previous question. If the motion to table carries, propositions go to the table as they are and when they come from the table the previous question is still in force and effect.

40. An affirmative vote on the motion for the previous question may be reconsidered if no vote has been taken under the previous question.

A motion to reconsider the vote on the previous question may be made only once.

Questions of Order

41. If the chair submits the question of order to the assembly for decision, it takes the same standing as an appeal and is debatable or not as an appeal on the ruling would be debatable. (See "Debatable" under "Appeal.")

42. The motion to lay on the table may be made while a question of order is pending. It applies to the main question and if adopted carries the question of order to the table with the main question.

43. If the question of order is submitted to the assembly and is debatable, the previous question can be applied.

44. If a question of order is given to the assembly for decision, the vote of the assembly may be reconsidered.

Ratify

45. See "Motions Applicable" in Section 185, p. 197-8.

46. The motion to ratify is adopted by a majority vote unless the rules of the organization or the rules of the parent organization of which it is a part specify another vote for adoption.

Reconsider

47. When a motion to reconsider is pending and the motion to lay on the table is made and adopted, the motion to table carries the motion to reconsider as well as the proposition sought to be reconsidered to the table.

48. When a motion to postpone to a certain time is made to apply to the motion to reconsider, the motion to postpone, if adopted, postpones the motion to reconsider and the proposition sought to be reconsidered together.

49. The vote on a motion to reconsider may be reconsidered if the proposition was amended materially at the time of the first reconsideration.

Rescind

50. An affirmative vote on the motion to rescind cannot be reconsidered.

51. If notice has been given of the motion to rescind, a majority vote will adopt. Without notice a two-thirds vote or a majority vote of the entire membership is necessary.

Motion to Make a Special Order

52. The motion to table the main proposition may be made while the motion to postpone and the amendment to make it a special order are pending, and if adopted, carries the motion to postpone and the amendment to it to the table with the main proposition. Likewise when the incidental motion to set as a special order is pending and a motion to table the main question is made and adopted, the incidental motion to make a special order goes to the table with the main proposition.

53. An affirmative vote to set as a special order can be reconsidered, but a negative vote cannot.

54. An amendment to a motion to postpone to a certain time which would make the proposition postponed a special order is adopted by a majority vote even though the adoption of the motion as amended would require a two-thirds vote. When a motion

to set as a special order is an incidental motion, it requires a two-thirds vote for adoption.

Amend Standing Rules

55.   Standing rules may be amended or rescinded at any meeting by majority vote provided a notice of the proposed action was given. If notice was not given, the amendment or rescission requires a two-thirds vote.

Take a Recess

56.   When the time arrives for taking a recess which has been provided for in the order of business, the assembly may postpone the time of taking the recess by a two-thirds vote.

Withdrawal of a Motion

57.   An affirmative vote on withdrawal of a motion cannot be reconsidered.

INDEX